Managing the Equity Factor

MANAGING THE EQUITY FACTOR

Or "After All I've Done for You . . ."

Richard C. Huseman, Ph.D.

John D. Hatfield, Ph.D.

HOUGHTON MIFFLIN COMPANY · BOSTON

1989

Copyright © 1989 by Richard C. Huseman and John D. Hatfield

ALL RIGHTS RESERVED

For information about permission to reproduce selections from this book, write
to Permissions, Houghton Mifflin Company, 2 Park Street,
Boston, Massachusetts 02108.

The quotation from *Pygmalion* by George Bernard Shaw on page 67 is reprinted
by permission of The Society of Authors on behalf of the
Bernard Shaw Estate.

Library of Congress Cataloging-in-Publication Data

Huseman, Richard C.
Managing the equity factor, or "After all I've done for you — " /
Richard C. Huseman, John D. Hatfield.
p. cm.
Bibliography: p.
ISBN 0-395-49167-3
1. Interpersonal relations. 2. Fairness. 3. Employee motivation —
United States. 4. Employee morale — United States. I. Hatfield,
John D., date. II. Title.
HM132.H865 1989
158'.2 — dc 19 88-27572
CIP

Printed in the United States of America

Q 10 9 8 7 6 5 4 3 2 1

Contents

Preface

This book is about influencing people.
"After All I've Done for You . . ." is a phrase that captures
our disappointment when we suddenly discover that we
don't have the influence to get what we thought we could
count on from others.

**This book is designed for anyone who wants to in-
fluence people and manage relationships better in a
variety of settings.**
At work, your approach to managing relationships
strongly affects your influence with individual people
both above and below you. **At home**, your approach to
managing relationships with your spouse, children, and
even friends can improve the health of those relationships
and the satisfaction you get from them.

**This book is based upon the single most powerful
element in effective relationship management—the
Equity Factor.**
As you read this book, you'll discover a hidden system of
equity that guides and controls what people contribute to
relationships. And once you realize how the **Equity Factor** causes people to react and perform the way they do,

you will understand why they sometimes don't do what you expect or want them to.

This book will show you how the emerging "new management" is Relationship Management.
We believe that **at work** the greatest future increases in productivity will come not from innovation or new technologies, but from *employees themselves.* **At home,** more productive and satisfying relationships will come from helping others get what they want and need from their relationships with you.

Using the strategies we set forth in the **Equity Power Paradigm,** you will be better able to influence and motivate people in all kinds of arenas, ranging from multinational corporations to family businesses . . . and even to families themselves. The strategies also apply to all levels of management—executive or middle management, line supervision, and even one-on-one relationships.

This book will help you manage the Equity Factor.
It will put you in a position to say *less often* . . .
"After All I've Done for You."

Richard C. Huseman
John D. Hatfield
Athens, Georgia

Managing the Equity Factor

Charlie's Story

We were flying from Atlanta to Pittsburgh. The stranger seated across the aisle from us was about sixty. He appeared unusually tired and deeply troubled.

He told us his name was Charlie. A business consultant with a major consulting firm, Charlie had worked with organizations throughout the world, and by most standards he was quite successful.

When Charlie asked where we were headed, we told him Toronto, where we were scheduled to give a seminar. He asked what the seminar was about, and we gave him our title—"After All I've Done for You . . ." Charlie repeated the title out loud. "That's the story of my life," he said quietly. For the next hour, we heard Charlie's story.

And as he talked about his wife, his daughter, and his dog, we understood why the phrase "After All I've Done for You . . ." had special meaning for him.

Charlie's Wife

As Charlie talked about his relationship with his wife, he openly admitted that he traveled a lot, was often not home on weekends, and sometimes forgot a birthday or an anniversary. But he had worked hard at his profession and made many important contributions to his marriage—a large paycheck, a swimming pool in the back yard, two cars, and an occasional vacation to some exotic getaway where only the "rich and famous" seem to go.

You can imagine Charlie's surprise when he returned home from a business trip one Friday evening to find that his wife had moved out. At the divorce hearing Charlie learned that his wife of twenty-seven years had wanted not more of his money, but more of his time.

Charlie's Daughter

Charlie also thought that he had made significant contributions to his relationship with his daughter. When she was a child, he always returned home from his travels with a gift for her. He delighted in seeing her tiny face burst into a smile as she opened his present.

Naturally, Charlie sometimes felt guilty about being away from home on business so much while his daughter was growing up. But he reasoned that his travels would help him earn the money for her college education. In fact, when the time came, Charlie's daughter did attend a rather expensive school at that. Charlie thought that he had prepared financially. But the more money he sent to his daughter, the more she seemed to need. His plight became almost unbearable when his daughter moved out of her $325-a-semester dorm room and into a $400-a-month apartment, instructing the landlord to send her monthly bill for the rent to good old Charlie.

Charlie said that he attended his daughter's college graduation with tears in his eyes, not because he was especially happy that she'd finally received her degree after five and a half years, but more because he was thinking about the thousands of dollars he still owed for her college education!

When we asked how his daughter was doing now, Charlie spoke softly, telling us that he didn't really know. "We haven't talked to each other in over three years."

Charlie's Dog

As part of his divorce settlement, Charlie sold his home and divided the proceeds with his former wife. He rented an apartment and bought a dog for $500. Of course the $500 purchase price for his new companion was just the beginning, followed by trips to a veterinarian who seemed to be more expensive than most medical doctors. There were also obedience training, pet sitters to take care of his dog when Charlie was out of town, and a host of other expenses that Charlie hadn't anticipated. But Charlie's relationship with his dog ended abruptly one night when he returned home from a business trip. As he opened the door and entered his apartment, Charlie's $500-plus dog dashed over and bit him on the leg. The next day Charlie sold his dog.

As our plane landed in Pittsburgh, we asked Charlie where he was headed. He said that he was checking into a psychiatric hospital for observation. It seems that after all Charlie had done for his company, Charlie's superiors thought he was suffering from burnout and needed a leave of absence. After the doctors observed him for a few days, Charlie hoped they'd have some advice about how he could cure his depression.

At age sixty, Charlie is alone . . . puzzled about life and troubled about relationships that somehow didn't work out. Perhaps you can understand why the phrase "After

All I've Done for You . . ." struck such a responsive chord in him.

But Charlie certainly isn't alone.

CONSIDER . . .

Each day across this country 50,000 people quit their jobs. Some are moving to better jobs. Many are not. And these statistics ignore still other people who have also "quit" their jobs but keep coming to work. In fact, in a recent survey of workers across the United States, nearly 85% said that they could work harder on the job. More than half claimed they could *double* their effectiveness "if I wanted to."

CONSIDER . . .

Each day across this country 2,122 marriages end in divorce. For every two marriages that begin a new relationship, divorce ends a third. We wonder how many couples have "divorced" but continue to live together. In fact, studies show that in a "happy" marriage, husbands and wives talk to each other an average of fifteen minutes a *week*. This talking doesn't include everyday comments, such as "pass the bacon" or "where's the newspaper," but serious conversations about their relationship and what they each want from it. And during those precious fifteen minutes, seven out of ten statements made are negative. "So you overdrew the checking account again!" "Why do I always have to take the kids to school?" "How long is your mother going to stay?"

CONSIDER . . .

Each day across this country 1,380 teenage children run away from home. Many of them are never heard from again. We don't know, of course, how many teenagers have run away emotionally but continue to live in tense and antagonistic relationships with their parents.

Perhaps you don't fall into one of these statistical categories. We also hope that you don't have a lot in common with Charlie. But the real tragedy is that:

- It's not our intentions that cause problems. We want to manage productive employees. We want to have satisfying marriages. We want to enjoy good relationships with our children.
- It's not that we don't try. We spend untold hours thinking about, worrying over, and getting advice about our important life relationships.
- It's what we *don't know* that causes us to *do what we should not do* and *not do what we should do* to have more productive, more satisfying relationships in life.

As you read the pages that follow, you'll come to a new understanding of why people at work and people at home perform and react the way they do. As you'll discover, the single most powerful principle for managing productive people at work and having healthy relationships at home is what we call the **Equity Factor.**

You'll also discover practical, everyday strategies for putting the Equity Factor to work in your relationships. At the office, these strategies will help you manage employees better so that they make more significant contributions to your organization because they *want* to. At home, these strategies will help you develop a more satisfying relationship with your spouse.

Be warned. Much of what we'll present in this book is *not* based upon the so-called golden rule—"Do unto others as you would have them do unto you." We'll show you later how applying the golden rule literally in relationships can create more problems than you ever imagined.

Be warned. The Equity Factor is the most important factor in relationships. Yet the Equity Factor and its accompanying strategies do not support the old adage that "It's more blessed to give than to receive." As you'll find out, in productive relationships it's blessed *both* to give *and* to receive.

Be warned. It isn't your intentions, your effort, or the amount of time you contribute to relationships that counts. Instead, it's the other person's *perception* of these and the other contributions you make. In the case of relationships, beauty really *is* in the eye of the beholder.

First, then, we'll explore the **Equity Factor** and its impact on relationships. Second, we'll help you see why others might not understand or appreciate your contributions to a relationship. Third, we'll identify some specific reasons why relationships are difficult to manage and how people tend to do the wrong things with the right intentions. Finally, we'll show you how to begin using relationship management strategies that apply the **Equity Power Paradigm.** In doing so, you'll be on the receiving side of more productive and more satisfying relationships with the important people in your life.

1

The Equity Factor

Give me that which I want, and you shall have that which you want.

ADAM SMITH

We were standing in line at the Atlanta airport waiting to have our baggage checked. We noticed that some people ahead of us gave the skycap a dollar or two as they asked him to handle their baggage carefully or make sure it got on the right plane. But the man standing just in front of us took a different approach. He didn't offer a tip, but he sternly lectured the skycap about taking special care of his two bags. He swore loudly when one of his bags tipped over accidentally, then angrily stalked off toward his gate.

As we stepped up to take our turn, the skycap's broad grin caught our attention. We asked him how he was able to keep smiling given the sometimes difficult people he had to serve. "What do you mean?" he asked. "That fellow who just swore at you," we replied. The skycap smiled again. "Oh, that dude? People like him are easy. You see, he's heading for L.A., but his bags are going to Detroit!"

A basic principle in human relationships is that people give to get. That's why when you open a door for someone, you expect a simple thank-you or a smile in return. It's also why you anticipate greater commitment from an

7

employee after you've given him a bonus. And it's the reason you hope that your spouse might overlook your arriving home late because you were on time three nights in a row last week.

The phrase "After All I've Done for You . . ." is a simple, outward expression of an inner feeling that what you have given does not equal what you have received in return. You feel shortchanged in the relationship. Beneath this feeling lies the most powerful principle of human behavior—the Equity Factor.

The Roots of Equity

Whether he realized it or not, the skycap we mentioned earlier was reacting to the Equity Factor, which has a rich history in philosophy, economics, anthropology, and psychology. In fact, the notion of equity was first set forth more than two thousand years ago. In his *Nicomachean Ethics*, Aristotle left little doubt that what people give and get is at the core of human relationships: "The very existence of the state depends on reciprocity . . . it is exchange that binds men together."

Our inclination to "give to get" is also reflected in eighteenth- and nineteenth-century economic history, in which the names John Stuart Mill, Adam Smith, and Jeremy Bentham are prominent. In the *Wealth of Nations* Adam Smith tells us: "It is not from the benevolence of the butcher, the brewer, or the baker that we expect our dinner, but from their regard to their own interest."

You'll see Smith's notion of exchange in modern advertising slogans. The Sears Discover card is "For People Who Expect Value." Chevrolet's Nova "Gives So Much and Asks So Little in Return." And Diners Club urges you to "Join the Club. The Rewards Are Endless."

One of the most unusual examples of how people give to get in relationships was reported by anthropologist Bronislaw Malinowski in the early 1920s. While studying the Trobriand Islanders in the South Seas, Malinowski discovered that the inhabitants of these islands had created an intriguing circle of exchange among themselves: the Kula Ring.

Islanders in the Kula Ring exchanged two items, armlets and necklaces. Armlets traveled in one direction around the ring and throughout the islands. Necklaces moved in the opposite direction. In any exchange, people always traded an armlet for a necklace.

Malinowski distinguished this unique trading network from economic exchange. The Kula Ring was meant to cement the bonds of social rather than economic relationships among the islanders. The rule was "once in the Kula, always in the Kula." The Kula Ring was a lifelong relationship.

Modern-day psychologists have found that we are similar to the Trobriand Islanders. In our life relationships, we exchange far more than just money. And we keep track of what we trade. This is the general notion of equity. And here is how it works in your relationships.

The Equity Factor in Relationships

As managers, we want employees to be productive and committed. But we are often disappointed when they arrive late for work, take extended breaks and lunch hours, and call in sick even though we're sure that they're not. We wonder why they sometimes pad their expense accounts, take company property home for their personal use, and even commit acts of sabotage. And we are frequently dismayed when they suddenly quit their jobs and go to work for our competitors.

As spouses, we want happy and satisfying marriages. But we are often disappointed when our spouse breaks an important promise or walks out during an argument. We wonder why our spouse pays so little attention to us anymore or why he or she seems to forget anniversaries or birthdays. And we are dismayed when our spouse "quits" our marriage and perhaps moves in with someone else.

If you understand the Equity Factor, then you'll see why many of these unpleasant events take place in people's relationships at work and at home. You'll also know what to do to avoid such disappointments in your own relationships. So let's get started.

Think about one important relationship you have— with a subordinate, your boss, your spouse, or perhaps one of your children.

On the left-hand side of the next page, draw up a list of all the contributions you are making to this relationship— what you are giving. With a subordinate, your contributions might include pay, job security, time, and professional development. With a spouse, you might list love, respect, trust, and emotional support. Make your list as lengthy as you can. Notice that this list is titled "What I Give."

On the right-hand side of the page, make a second list, "What I Get." Write down all the benefits that you are receiving from your relationship. Time? Loyalty? Advice? Make this list lengthy, too, if you can.

Now sit back and compare your two lists. Don't count the number of items on each one. Some things are more important than others. And you've probably left some items off both lists. Instead, answer this simple question:

What I Give	What I Get

Considering all that you give to your relationship versus all that you're getting from it, who is getting the better deal? Choose one from the following three options:

- I'm getting a better deal.
- The other person is getting a better deal.
- We're getting an equally good deal.

We'll now analyze your answer by looking at what we call the three Axioms of Equity. As we do, you'll better understand why you behave the way you do in your relationships, and why others do or don't do for you.

Equity Axiom 1

People Evaluate Their Relationships by Comparing What They Give to a Relationship with What They Get from It.

What you contribute to relationships ("What I Give") is called **Inputs**. What you receive ("What I Get") is called **Outcomes**. Moments ago when you compared what you gave to your relationship to what you got from it, you were evaluating your Inputs versus your Outcomes.

Picture a tiny, computerlike device in the back of your mind. This computer keeps track of both what you contribute to major relationships in your life and what you receive from them. It begins operating when you are very young and functions until the day you leave this world. You can never really turn the computer off. It continues to run, adding new Inputs and Outcomes, changing their importance, and sometimes removing them, all of the time calculating and recalculating your **Equity Score.**

Equity Axiom 1

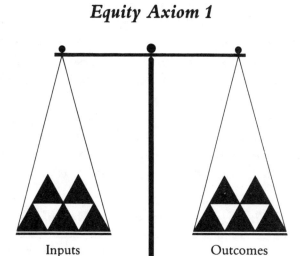

Inputs   Outcomes

People evaluate relationships by comparing what they give to a relationship with what they get from it.

Usually, the computer operates at a subconscious level, and you're not even aware of its existence. But if Inputs and Outcomes get out of balance, then that computer will very clearly point out your Equity Score right away.

So what's your Equity Score for the relationship you were thinking of a few minutes ago? If your answer was "I'm getting the better deal," then you are **Over-Rewarded** in your relationship: your Outcomes exceed your Inputs. If you answered, "The other person is getting a better deal," then you are **Under-Rewarded** because your Inputs are greater than your Outcomes. And if your answer was "We are getting an equally good deal," then you are **Equitably Rewarded** in your relationship: Inputs are fairly equal to Outcomes.

During the past few years, we've asked several thousand people in some of America's largest corporations to tell us who's getting the better deal—they or the organization for which they work. As you can see in the chart below, over half of the managers in the organizations we surveyed feel Under-Rewarded. What's perhaps even more troubling is that more than 80% of hourly employees feel that their employer is getting the better deal.

Who Has Equity in the Workplace

	Managers	Hourlies
Feel Over-Rewarded	13%	7%
Feel Equitably Rewarded	34%	10%
Feel Under-Rewarded	53%	83%

Like these managers and hourly employees, you can and do compare your Inputs to your Outcomes in life relationships. Yet psychologists aren't really sure how you make the actual comparison. Some claim that you do so in relation to someone else in a position or situation similar to yours. For example, you might think that you are underpaid for the amount of work you do because a co-worker does less work but is paid the same salary as you.

Others think that you compare your Inputs and Outcomes against a standard that earlier life experiences have written into your mind. If you have been married more than once, then you might evaluate the Inputs and Outcomes in your current marriage against what you gave and received (or didn't) in a previous marriage. Or perhaps you feel Under-Rewarded for the work you do because an earlier job paid just as well as your present one, but you're now working much harder and for longer hours.

Still others believe that you compare your Inputs and Outcomes to what the other person in your relationship appears to be giving and getting. Thus, you might feel a bit Over-Rewarded because that person puts more time and effort into your relationship but gets less from you in return.

What we *do* know is that people evaluate relationships by comparing their Inputs to their Outcomes. This comparison creates one of three feelings: Over-Reward, Equitable Reward, or Under-Reward. We also know that many people in typical organizations feel a strong sense of Under-Reward. Obviously, only you know how you feel about the relationship you evaluated earlier.

But what's more important is how people *react* to feelings of Over-Reward and Under-Reward. This leads us to Equity Axiom 2.

Equity Axiom 2

When What People Give to a Relationship Does Not Equal What They Get from It, They Feel Distress.

The distress you feel in inequitable relationships comes in two forms. Over-Rewarded people tend to feel guilt. Under-Rewarded people experience resentment.

The Guilt of Over-Reward

Have you ever received too much change after a purchase in a department store, but you didn't realize it until you were in your car? Have you received a lavish gift from a friend for whom you did a small favor? If so, then you know how it feels to be Over-Rewarded. The guilt of Over-Reward is used in some ingenious ways:

- Sellers of vacation property give you one of three grand prizes in a special drawing. Your only obligation is to visit the property to pick up your prize. And while you're there, you'll probably feel a bit guilty unless you listen to a sales pitch on the property as well.
- Charitable organizations send you stamps, address labels, or other small gifts. Their only request is that you make a donation in return. Some of us, of course, ignore their request for money. But the guilt of Over-Reward compels others to donate money, throw the gift away, or perhaps even give the gift to someone else.
- Some organizations send surveys with a request that you fill them out. Most of these surveys wind up in the trash can. Other organizations send a half dollar or even an entire dollar with the survey. Many of these surveys are completed and returned. In fact, an executive who conducts surveys of retail store owners told us about one retailer who returned his uncompleted survey, the dollar, and a letter of apology for not having the time to complete the survey. The survey would have taken no more than two minutes to complete. We wonder how long it took the retailer to write his letter?

One of our favorite examples of the guilt of Over-Reward was reported by two university professors. Several years ago these professors sent Christmas cards to 528 total strangers. More than one hundred of their surprised recipients of a Christmas greeting responded with either a Christmas card of their own, an entire letter, or, incredibly enough, a telephone call. While most of the returning cards contained only a signature, many others included handwritten notes about their family or recalling old friendships with these two professors. Some people even included pictures of their families, pets, and friends. But only six Christmas card recipients said that they couldn't remember the professors and asked for more information! We do try to keep things balanced in relationships, and the guilt of Over-Reward causes some interesting reactions.

The Resentment of Under-Reward

Our responses to the guilt of Over-Reward are often unusual and amusing. But what we need to be concerned about is the second form of distress—the resentment of Under-Reward. You might recall that 53% of managers and 83% of hourly employees feel Under-Rewarded in relation to their organizations. Some probably are only a bit irritated by this situation. Others are genuinely angry. In fact, the Under-Rewarded people in these organizations report that they are significantly less satisfied in their jobs than their Equitably Rewarded counterparts. People who are Over-Rewarded in relationships try to remove their burden of guilt in often unpredictable ways. But people who feel the resentment and frustration of Under-Reward react predictably—and decisively. This leads us to our final Equity Axiom.

Equity Axiom 3

*People Who Feel Distress in Relationships
Because They Give More Than They Get
Will Restore Equity.*

"After All I've Done for You . . ." is a phrase that says,
"Look at my Inputs to our relationship" and a sign that
someone feels badly Under-Rewarded. When people feel
the resentment of Under-Reward, they will restore equity
in one of three ways.

I. REDUCING INPUTS

Think about a relationship in which you experienced the
frustration of Under-Reward. Did you contribute less
to the relationship? In organizations, Under-Rewarded
people will often simply reduce their contributions by:

- coming to work late
- doing less work
- doing careless work
- calling in sick
- taking extended breaks and lunch hours
- "forgetting" to carry out instructions
- sabotaging their work and the work of others

It's not difficult for people to think of ways they've re-
stored equity in work relationships. An executive once
told us about his resentment at being passed over for an
important promotion. He decided to find another job.
But while he was looking for that job, he simply sat
around in his office, doing as little as possible. He says
that he felt a certain sense of satisfaction when he finally

resigned three months later, because in some small way he had evened the score.

Another person described his high school summer job working in a peach-packing shed. His job was to top off each basket with the best peaches that he selected from a conveyor belt. Doing so would mean that peach buyers who opened the baskets to inspect them would think that each basket contained only the finest peaches. When he and two coworkers were angered by having to work until midnight three days in a row, the three of them began topping off randomly chosen baskets with small, bruised, and even rotten peaches. Although he feels guilty today about engaging in this act of sabotage, he and his co-workers felt enormous satisfaction at the owner's embarrassment when buyers claimed that the company was trying to sell bad peaches.

Even professional baseball players sometimes reduce their Inputs to restore equity. Some years ago a study of players in their free agency year (the final year of their contract) discovered that many players were having down years in which batting averages, runs batted in, and other measures of a player's effectiveness dropped. You'd think that they would try harder during their free agency year so as to have more leverage when bargaining with a new team. But the researchers who conducted the study concluded that a subconscious desire to restore equity for low salaries in the past was much stronger than a conscious wish to have a good year to improve their bargaining position.

People who feel Under-Rewarded in marriages restore equity by:

- spending less time with their spouse
- forgetting important anniversaries, birthdays, and other special occasions
- neglecting minor household chores they've agreed to handle
- withholding compliments and other forms of healthy communication
- refusing to try to resolve conflicts

Thus, a general pattern of neglect and noninvolvement is one means by which Under-Rewarded spouses seek to regain equity in their marriage relationship. Their approach is simply "I'll do less until you do more."

2. INCREASING OUTCOMES

People who feel Under-Rewarded can also try to change their Outcomes from a relationship. At work, people will ask for:

- pay raises
- promotions
- increased job security
- more benefits
- transfers to different jobs
- better working conditions

If their requests aren't granted, employees might increase their Outcomes in other ways—taking company property home, padding expense accounts, and doing other things that don't actually even the score but nevertheless make them feel a sense of equity. An executive recently told us of her outrage at discovering that the salary of one of her new subordinates was $2,300 a year more than hers. She immediately confronted her plant manager. He confirmed that she was, indeed, making less money than her subordinate. However, he couldn't do anything about her problem because the company simply had to "pay more to get good people these days." Several weeks later she quit her job. As she was emptying her desk, she slipped a dictionary that belonged to her employer into her briefcase. "I'd never stolen anything in my life," she told us. "But for some reason, I just picked it up and carried it out." As she passed through security, she was terrified that someone might want to check the contents of her briefcase. But no one did. And today the company's dictionary gathers dust on a shelf in her study. She calls it her "$2,300 dictionary."

People who feel Under-Rewarded in marriage increase their Outcomes by demanding:

- more time with their spouse
- more affection
- more control in decision-making
- more credit for their Inputs
- more of anything that makes them feel a sense of equity

So when your spouse begins making what you might think are unreasonable requests, you are fairly safe in concluding that his or her demands are a way of saying, "After all I've done for you, I expect something more out of this relationship."

3. ENDING THE RELATIONSHIP
The third way that Under-Rewarded people restore equity is simply to end the relationship. As we told you earlier, each day across this country:

- 50,000 people quit their jobs
- 2,122 marriages end in divorce
- 1,380 teenagers run away from home

Quitting a job, filing for divorce, or running away from home obviously doesn't bring equity back into the relationship. But for some angry and frustrated people, there appears to be no better option. They feel the distress of being shortchanged in an important life relationship. Their efforts to restore equity have been unsuccessful. Why not leave before the inequity becomes even greater?

A summary of the three Axioms of Equity appears on the next page. What these axioms tell us is that people want equity in their relationships with superiors, subordinates, coworkers, their organizations, spouses, children, and even friends. When they feel inequity, they'll do everything in their power to restore the balance between what they give to and what they get from the relationship, even if they must end the relationship to do so.

Equity Sensitivity

Perhaps you're bothered by the notion that people always expect something in return for their contributions to a relationship. "That's not me," you might be saying. "I give a lot and expect little in return."

During the past several years we've discovered exceptions to the Equity Axioms. In fact, we developed a little test we call the Equity Sensitivity Test. Having given this test to nearly four thousand people, we can safely tell you that some people, in fact, want to give more than they get. We call these people **Benevolents**. Others unfortunately prefer to get more than they give. We call them **Entitleds**. But most people do look for a balance between

The Equity Factor

Axiom 1

People Evaluate Relationships by Comparing What They *Give* to a Relationship with What They *Get* from It.

Axiom 2

When What People Give Does Not Equal What They Get, They Feel *Distress*.

Over-Reward = Guilt
Under-Reward = Resentment

Axiom 3

People Who Feel Distress Because They Give More Than They Get Will Restore Equity.

Reduce Inputs.
Increase Outcomes.
End the Relationship.

---

their Inputs and Outcomes. Most people are in the category we call **Equity Sensitives.**

Benevolents, who make up the smallest group of exceptions, prefer that their Inputs exceed their Outcomes for several reasons. Some are altruistic people who simply want to do for others, no matter what the return might be. Other Benevolents believe in a Calvinistic philosophy of high Inputs. Outcomes are not important. Still others give more than they get so that they can feel good about themselves. Benevolents are relationship givers.

Entitleds are relationship getters. Some Entitleds are members of the Me Generation, people who would rather get ahead *without* doing than get ahead *by* doing. Others are outgrowths of what some psychologists call "overly

The Equity Sensitivity Continuum

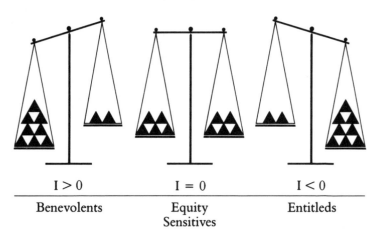

I > 0	I = 0	I < 0
Benevolents	Equity Sensitives	Entitleds

permissive child-rearing practices." In a recent study, preschool children were asked how many presents they expected to receive at Christmas. The average number they expected was just over three. Yet the actual number they received from their parents was more than eleven.

Perhaps a generation of Entitleds is being raised by well-meaning, Benevolent parents whose only wish is to give their children a better life than they themselves have had. In fact, our own studies show that younger people, especially college students, tend to be much more Entitled than the older generation of adults who've been in the workplace for a number of years.

Equity Sensitivity and Job Satisfaction

On a scale of 1 to 7 (with 7 being the highest), how satisfied are you in your current job? We've asked this question of just over 1,500 managers from across the United States. We also asked them the basic equity question: "Who's getting a better deal—you or the organization for which you work?" Then, using their responses to the Equity Sensitivity Test, we divided these managers into Benevolent, Entitled, and Equity Sensitive groups. The chart below shows the results of our study. The numbers for each of the nine groups are the average (from 1 to 7) job satisfaction scores for the managers who fell into each group.

Managers' Reactions to Equity and Inequity and Overall Job Satisfaction

	Under-Rewarded	Equitably Rewarded	Over-Rewarded
Benevolents	5.4	5.7	5.7
Equity Sensitives	4.9	5.5	5.1
Entitleds	4.6	4.9	5.2

Notice first that Benevolents are highly satisfied in their jobs even if they're Under-Rewarded. Entitleds are much harder to please. Even when Over-Rewarded, they are still not as satisfied (5.2) as Under-Rewarded Benevolents (5.4). Note also what happens to Over-Rewarded Equity Sensitives, and think back to what we told you about the guilt of Over-Reward.

So, the Equity Axioms don't apply equally to everybody. Some people are Benevolents who want their Inputs to exceed their Outcomes. Entitleds prefer just the opposite. And Equity Sensitives want Inputs and Outcomes to be in balance.

Further, it's likely that people don't approach all life relationships with the same orientation. Some people you know may be Benevolents at work and hard-nosed Entitleds at home. Whether or not they are, rest assured that people enter relationships with certain preferences for the balance between their Inputs and Outcomes. For most people, the inequity of Under-Reward will lead to attempts to regain a sense of equity in their relationships.

Equity is the fundamental, most powerful explanation for why people behave and react the way they do in relationships. It tells us why people are unproductive, unsatisfied, and uncommitted at work. It explains why many marriages are unsatisfying and unhappy. If you can manage equity, then you can get the results you want from important relationships in your life.

Managing equity, however, involves managing people's perceptions of what they give and get. In the next chapter, we'll see how perceptions of Inputs and Outcomes come about.

2

Eye of the Perceiver

The Prince and the Magician

Many years ago there was a young prince who believed in all things but three—princesses, islands, and God. His father, the king, had told him that these things did not exist. And because there were neither princesses nor islands nor any sign of God in the kingdom, the prince believed his father.

One day the young prince left his father's kingdom and traveled to a distant land. Standing on the coast of this land, he saw what appeared to be islands. On these islands he spied strange and beautiful creatures whom he dared not name. As the prince gazed at these creatures, a man in full evening dress approached.

"Are those real islands?" the young prince asked. "Of course they are," replied the man in evening dress. "And those strange and beautiful creatures?" asked the prince. The man smiled. "They are all genuine princesses." "Then God must also exist!" cried the prince. The man in full evening dress bowed. "I am God," he said.

The young prince rushed home to his father's kingdom. "So you are back," his father said. "Yes," the prince replied indignantly. "And I have seen islands and princesses. And I have also spoken to God." The king was unmoved.

"As I have told you before, such things simply don't exist."

"But I saw them!" the prince responded. "Then tell me how God was dressed," his father said. The prince thought for a moment and then answered, "God was in full evening dress." The king leaned forward. "And were the sleeves of his coat rolled back?" "Why, yes, they were," the prince said, remembering. The king smiled and spoke softly, "That is the uniform of a magician, my son. You have been deceived."

Disturbed by his father's statements, the young prince returned to the distant land, where he again stood upon the shore. As he looked once more at what appeared to be islands inhabited by princesses, the stranger in full evening dress reappeared. "My father, the king, has told me who you really are," said the prince, his voice filled with reproach. "I know that these are not real islands. Nor are those real princesses. Because you are not God. You are only a magician."

The man smiled. "It is your father who has deceived you, young prince. In his own kingdom there are many islands and many princesses. But you cannot see them because you are under your father's spell."

Deeply troubled, the young prince returned home. He went immediately to the king's chambers. "Father, is it true that you are a magician?" His father rolled back the sleeves of his robes. "Yes, my son, I am." "Then the man on the shore was, indeed, God," the prince said. "No," the king answered. "The man on the shore was only another magician."

The young prince cried out, "But I must know the truth . . . the truth beyond magic!" "There is no truth beyond magic," said the king. Filled with sadness, the prince spoke: "Then I will slay myself." By magic the king caused Death to appear at the prince's side. Death touched the prince's shoulder, and the prince shuddered, remembering the beautiful but unreal islands and the unreal but beautiful princesses.

"Very well," the prince said quietly. "I can bear it." Suddenly Death disappeared. The king placed his own hand on the prince's shoulder and spoke softly to him. "Now, my son, you too will be a magician."

In the world of relationships there is a bit of the prince and a bit of the magician in all of us. You've probably had experiences in relationships in which you've felt somewhat like the young prince trying desperately to understand the communication and the behavior of people around you. And if you've had trouble reconciling what people say with what they do, then you can perhaps identify with the prince's words: "I must know the truth . . . the truth beyond magic."

You've also probably played the part of magician in many of your relationships. You might have communicated with others or justified your own behavior in a strikingly similar manner to the magician king who told his son that real islands and real princesses don't exist. While few of us ever really try to convince others that islands and princesses are imaginary, we all at one time or another try to shape the perceptions of others in our relationships.

The story of the prince and the magician suggests that your world is not one of facts and reality but of *perceptions* of facts and reality. And your perceptions, the perceptions of others, and the real facts are rarely the same. Perhaps nowhere do these differences play a more important role than in human relationships, especially with regard to equity and your perceptions of equity. That's because there are three faces of equity in every relationship—your perception, the other person's perception, and, somewhere in between, reality.

The Three Faces of Equity

Harry had worked for his company for nearly twenty-four years. During those years, he had devoted long days and many weekends to his job. He'd been out of town much of the time and missed more family vacations than he'd been able to take. According to his wife, Harry was "married" to his job. That was exactly the way she put it when she asked for a separation two years ago. They had reconciled, but Harry's marriage hadn't really improved measurably.

Despite difficulties in his personal life, Harry was now within days of achieving his most significant professional goal, promotion to national sales manager. A senior vice president had told Harry confidentially that he was a leading contender for the position and that the company's president would make the announcement the following Monday. At last, Harry thought, his years of hard work and unselfish dedication would give him a much-needed edge for the national post.

Monday brought the announcement, but the job went to a person ten years Harry's junior. Angered and disappointed, Harry made an appointment with the president to find out why he'd been passed over. After all, he'd devoted his life to the company. In fact, his region had been tops in sales for the past four years.

The president was polite but firm: "The job's too big for you." Harry began to protest, but the president cut him off. "Harry, you know you have a tough time handling your own region. From what I hear, you're working nights and weekends. When's the last time you took a vacation with your family? No, this job's just too much for you to handle."

Harry walked slowly from the president's office. The words came easily: After All I've Done for Them. Yet the company president leaned back in his chair and thought, Someday he'll thank me for saving him from himself.

Think about the two entirely different views of equity in this relationship. One view is Harry's—passed over for promotion, his Inputs to the relationship either ignored or not appreciated. The other view is that of the president, whose Input to the relationship is saving a valued subordinate from destroying himself professionally. And somewhere in between are the facts as they really exist, unseen by either party.

You might recall that 53% of managerial and 83% of hourly employees in a number of large corporations report that they are Under-Rewarded. Are they? The facts might or might not confirm their perception. But their own superiors were baffled and disappointed to learn how they felt. And in this case, two sets of parties are thinking, "After All I've Done for You."

It's difficult to believe that so many people in organizations across this country are *actually* Under-Rewarded. In fact, they probably aren't. Feeling Under-Rewarded is only a perception—but a powerful one. You already know that this perception leads to resentment, followed by efforts to restore equity. But how is it that people so easily misunderstand or misinterpret the facts? How can they possibly think that they are treated so unfairly?

Let's see how these perceptions come about.

The World of Perception

A few months ago we were sitting in an airport between flights. Nearby were several airline employees discussing their relationship with management and a strike that had recently ended. One of the employees began a series of hostile statements about the airline by saying, "Yeah, and the last time they threw us out on strike . . ." We suspect that this airline's management would never "throw" anybody out on strike. But people do recall things in surprising ways.

The writer Aldous Huxley once stated that you are capable of accurately recalling *everything* that has ever happened to you and perceiving *everything* that is now happening in the universe. Obviously, recalling and perceiving everything would be overwhelming. Your mind would have so much information to process at one time that making sense out of any of it would be impossible.

Fortunately, nature has equipped you with certain *physical limitations* that help you sort through what is happening around you. Fortunately *and* unfortunately, you have developed *psychological limitations* that sometimes help and at other times hinder your ability to perceive the world accurately. Here's how these limitations work.

Physical Limitations: You perceive everything through one of five sense windows—sight, hearing, taste, touch, and smell. If your senses aren't impaired, they operate twenty-four hours a day. Consider what science tells you about these senses.

Light is a form of electromagnetic wave. Light waves travel through space at 186,000 miles a second. And you see light. Radar, radio signals, and x-rays are also electromagnetic waves. They also travel at 186,000 miles per second. But you don't see them. Although you might want to see radar signals transmitted from police cars, physical limitations don't allow you to do so. So you buy a radar detector, mount it on the dashboard of your car, and let it see for you.

The simple fact is that light waves account for less than 2% of all those electromagnetic waves rushing past you at this moment. Imagine how muddled your mind would be if you could see the electromagnetic waves emerging from radio stations in your community or the radar waves emitted from planes flying overhead.

Sound also travels in wave patterns. These wave patterns vibrate, and you hear them. "Normal" hearing means that you can hear sound waves that vibrate between 15 and 15,000 times a second. In older people who are experiencing a hearing loss, the upper limit drops to around 4,000. Among young children the upper limit can be as high as 30,000. Thus, they hear better than you do as an adult, although any parent will likely testify that his or her child is an exception!

If you could hear sound waves that vibrate fewer than 15 times per second, then, like the robin, you could hear earthworms moving beneath the ground. But you'd also hear your muscles expand and contract as you move your arms and legs. And you'd be plagued by the sound of your blood rumbling through your veins and arteries.

If there are bats in your neighborhood (or in your attic), then you'd be absolutely miserable if you could hear better than the normal human being. Bats find their way in the dark using a process called echo-location. They send out sound waves that vibrate between 50,000 and 90,000 times a second. These sound waves bounce off objects and back to the bats' ears. Bats use these echoes to locate things, such as cave walls, tiny insects, and your house.

Physical limitations affect your other senses as well. For

example, most birds have a wonderfully keen sense of hearing but almost no sense of smell. Yet the human sense of smell is finely developed, and often the only difference between French cuisine and an ordinary meal is the impact that food has on the olfactory receptors inside your nose. This is because you can taste only bitter, sweet, salty, and sour. Actually, when we eat, all five senses come together. Maybe that's why some of us enjoy mealtime so much.

So nature's physical limitations help us perceive better because we don't need to perceive everything. Although you might sometimes want to remove these limitations, they normally keep you from being overloaded with sensory information.

Psychological Limitations: More closely tied to your perception of equity in relationships are psychological limitations. These limitations are products of your individual, personal history. They may be based on heredity, your upbringing, where you've lived, where you went to school, a book you've read, a friend you've known, and on and on and on. Like fingerprints, psychological limitations are unique to every person. And they dramatically affect your perception of equity. Here's how.

Picture a medical doctor asleep in bed at home. It is well past midnight when the telephone rings. The doctor answers his phone, dresses, and leaves for the hospital. Yet his wife doesn't stir from her sleep. Two hours later the doctor returns home and climbs into bed with his still sleeping wife. He is soon fast asleep as well. But within an hour their newborn infant cries from her bedroom down the hall. The wife bolts upright. But the doctor doesn't stir.

You've already discovered that physical limitations keep you from being overloaded with sensory information.

But like the doctor and his wife, you also *learn* to attend to some things and ignore others. How do you decide what's important? For one thing, you pay more attention to anything related to your *personal goals and objectives.* That's why people who wear dentures watch denture-cleaner commercials on television more closely than people who still have their teeth (they pay more attention to toothpaste commercials). And dog owners attend to dog food commercials more often than people who don't have pets.

At work and at home, people pay attention to whatever relates to equity. That's because they've learned that a principal goal in life is maintaining a balance between Inputs and Outcomes. So at work they attend carefully to everything that might affect their Inputs and Outcomes: rumors about layoffs, pay raises, overtime, and who's getting promoted; memos describing increases or reductions in benefits or new policies on work hours. At home, they keep conscious and unconscious track of requests for favors, their spouses' behavior, and anything else that might affect equity in their relationship.

People attend to equity. But the cause of many problems is *how* they interpret what they pay attention to. That's why the facts would probably not confirm that 53% of managers and 83% of hourly employees are actually Under-Rewarded.

It's interesting how even simple words and phrases can bring about different reactions, depending on the psychological limitations you've developed. The chart on page 36, for example, lists some terms that management and labor often interpret quite differently.

In the world of perception, the same thing can mean entirely different things to different people. And too often

Perceptual Differences Between Management and Labor

Term	Meaning for Management	Meaning for Labor
Union	Trouble	Security
Labor agreement	Wall	Bridge
Overtime	Increased output	Lost free time
Recession	No pay raises	No job

we're disappointed when others don't seem to appreciate or understand what we've done for them. Equity is not a matter of facts or reality. Instead, it's a matter of fragile, peculiar, and sometimes slanted perceptions of reality.

Turkeys, Skunks, and Sharks

Roughly 1 out of 10 turkeys eaten in the United States this past Thanksgiving Day was raised in Oconee County, Georgia, about ten miles from where we live. If you ever visit a farm where turkeys are raised, then you'll discover that they aren't very intelligent birds. During rainstorms, some turkeys will tilt their heads back, open their beaks, and drink until they drown. When frightened during a thunderstorm, turkeys will scramble to the corner of their turkey house for protection. The problem is that they all tend to rush to the same corner, resulting, on occasion, in a pile of crushed, smothered turkeys. Now you know what it means when someone calls you a "turkey."

Despite their lack of intelligence, female turkeys tend to be good mothers. They're very watchful and protective of their young, spending much of their time warming their chicks beneath their wings. This mothering behavior is apparently triggered by a distinctive, high-pitched "cheep cheep" sound that young turkeys (poults) make.

Other identifying features of turkey poults—smell, appearance, and touch—appear to play almost no role in causing this protective behavior from the mother turkey. In fact, if a baby turkey for some reason fails to make that "cheep cheep" sound, then its mother will abandon it, or, in some cases, kill it.

The mother turkey's nearly total reliance on a single behavior—the baby chick's making that "cheep cheep" sound—to identify her young was reported by animal behaviorist M. S. Fox in his description of an experiment involving mother turkeys and a stuffed skunk. Skunks are a natural enemy of turkeys, and whenever a skunk approaches, the mother turkey will flap her wings, squawk, and peck and claw at the skunk to drive it away. Fox reported that even a stuffed skunk, pulled by a string toward a mother turkey, triggered this same violent reaction. The mother turkey would attack the skunk immediately and viciously, *until* the researchers turned on a tiny tape recorder inside the stuffed skunk, a recorder that made a simple sound—"cheep cheep." Hearing this sound, the mother turkey would not only cease her attack, but occasionally try to draw the skunk protectively under her wing. But when the tape recorder was turned off, the mother turkey would renew her attack.

Fox's study showed how the mother turkey focuses almost entirely on one behavior and generalizes from that sound, sometimes incorrectly. If you enjoy turkey dinners, then you should be grateful that living skunks can't make anything close to a "cheep cheep" sound. You should also be thankful that, as a human being, you are able to think, understand, and perceive the world around you better than any mother turkey.

But having the ability to perceive doesn't always translate to accurate perceptions. Consider the following four questions.

QUESTION 1: **How many people in the United States die each year of skin cancer?** 7,500—yet most of us continue to sunbathe.

QUESTION 2: **How many people in the United States die each year in auto accidents?** Nearly 50,000—yet 92% of the adult population continues to drive.

QUESTION 3: **How many people in the United States die each year of diseases related to smoking?** Nearly 150,000—yet 38% of the adult population continues to smoke.

QUESTION 4: **How many swimmers die each year from shark attacks?** 2—worldwide.

Next time you're near the ocean, walk down to the beach armed with these statistics. Step carefully over all the people lying there soaking up the sun's rays. Wade into the surf until it gets about knee-high. Then, at the top of your lungs, yell two words—not "cheep cheep" but "Shark! Shark!" Then stand back and watch the "turkeys"

- scramble out of the water
- stumble over the sunbathers
- jump into their cars
- light up a cigarette
- drive to safety

People are susceptible to what we call Shark Syndrome Perception. Despite a finely developed human capacity for understanding the world around them, people often perceive only what they want to perceive in their relationships, no matter what the facts say and despite the other party's efforts to convince them otherwise.

In the next chapter, we'll explore four specific reasons why equity is difficult to manage in relationships. You'll discover that these reasons often grow from misperceptions people have about the relationship, "Shark Syndrome Perception."

3

Why Equity in Relationships Is Difficult to Manage

Think back to your first day on the job. Chances are you had very positive expectations—the very best in terms of salary increases, advancement in the organization, job security, and job satisfaction. The frustrations of someone else getting credit for your work or the promotion you wanted, the hardship of dealing with difficult people, or the possibility of actually losing your job were not among your expectations that first day.

Think back to the day you were married. Chances are you had very positive expectations that day—the best in terms of happiness, love, perhaps children, financial security, and growing old with someone you cherished. The frustrations of illness, a two-career family, teenage children, or financial difficulty were not among your expectations that first day.

Think back to the day your first child was born. Chances are you had very positive expectations—the best in terms of your child's becoming successful and talented, well educated, perhaps athletic, and a source of immense pride. The frustrations of a teenager who stayed out late at night and was involved with drugs or alcohol, of seemingly endless conflicts at the dinner table, or of a son or daughter who had no career goals after college were not among your expectations on that special day. We begin most relationships with high expectations. But changes take place between our expectations at the beginning and the frustration and disappointment we too often feel later. Relationships *are* difficult to manage, at least to manage well. And the trouble we have in relationships can be traced to how we manage (or mismanage) equity. Here, then, are four reasons why equity in relationships is difficult to manage.

Why Equity Is Difficult to Manage

1. The Wrong Psychological Currency

Not to get what you want is almost the same as not to get anything at all.

ARISTOTLE

How much is one dollar worth? That dollar will probably buy you the same cup of coffee in California as it will in Florida. The exchange rate is the same on the East and West coasts. When you travel to a foreign country, the exchange rate is usually fixed as well. One dollar will get you 200 pesos, 2.8 marks, 9 francs, and so on, depending on the exchange rate that day. In economic transactions, the currencies are tangible and the rate of exchange is fixed. In relationships we exchange currencies as well. But most of these relationship currencies are not tangible, and the exchange rate is rarely fixed.

Earlier in this book you met Charlie, a busy executive who arrived home one Friday night expecting a customary "welcome home" greeting from his wife. Instead, his wife ended their relationship. Charlie is not unlike many people—men *and* women—in organizations across America. They work long days and nights and even longer weekends so that their family can have those extras that money can buy. Like Charlie, they discover too late that what their family wanted was not more of their money but more of their time. These well-meaning people offer what we call the **Wrong Psychological Currency**.

The first reason why equity in relationships is difficult to manage is that the currencies we provide—our inputs to the relationship—are either misunderstood or not appreciated by the other person because they are the wrong currencies.

Earlier we asked you to make a list of your Inputs and Outcomes in an important relationship in your life. Check your list. Are you certain that the Inputs you listed are actually valued by the other person? Unfortunately, there are countless examples of people making what *they* think are important contributions to relationships, contributions that require a lot of effort. Then they discover that the other person simply doesn't value or appreciate what they've done:

- An employee arrives at work thirty minutes early every day and stays after work every night, but gets little credit because his supervisor is interested not in the number of hours worked, but in the amount of work done.
- An executive thinks that company morale problems can be solved through pay raises, but is disappointed

when his problems don't disappear in "a puff of green smoke."

- A manager treats her employees warmly and considerately but receives little respect from them because she lacks the courage to terminate unproductive people.
- A college student earns good grades, is involved in campus activities, and avoids drugs and alcohol, but his relationship with his parents is strained because he doesn't attend church regularly.
- A dedicated homemaker spends hours preparing lavish meals for her family, but can't understand why her sons are never on time for dinner.

During the past few years we have identified the most important Outcomes people want from their jobs. Listed below, in rank order with 1 being the most important, are the top five.

1. A sense of accomplishment
2. Recognition for good work
3. Competitive pay
4. Making use of one's abilities
5. Challenging work

These are the "right" psychological currencies for much of this nation's work force. Yet how many jobs actually offer these Outcomes? If you've ever experienced assembly line work, then you'll understand why people are sometimes paid so much to do it. The work is generally unchallenging and mind-numbing, and the only sense of accomplishment many assembly line workers experience is surviving to the end of their shift. Fortunately, most managerial positions offer healthy doses of these Outcomes, despite the fact that recognition for good work, as we'll show you later, is a rare Outcome for both managerial and nonmanagerial employees in many organizations.

Note critically that these and other Outcomes employees want from their jobs are also Inputs that you can provide; with employees *your* Inputs to the relationship are *their* Outcomes. Likewise, many of their Inputs (for example, quantity and quality of work) are Outcomes for you.

In terms of the Outcomes employees provide for you, be aware also that many people view such things as their educational background, age, seniority, and the skills they bring to the job as actual Inputs to the relationship. Although you might perceive job performance as the right psychological currency, some people who work for you think that you should appreciate them for who they are as well. And they're disappointed when you don't.

We have the same currency problems in marriages. Studies show that important Outcomes in marital relationships include trust, love, respect, communication, and listening. Yet too many of us would rather provide money and other tangible goods than the psychological currencies our spouse really wants.

The Golden Rule in Relationships

One reason we often give the wrong psychological currency is that we have learned to apply the golden rule faithfully—"**Do unto others as you would have them do unto you.**" But too often we have little evidence that what we want is what others also want. A better prescription for managing equity in relationships and engaging in the right psychological currency is to modify the golden rule—**"Do unto others as they would have you do unto them."**

Thus, before you invest time, energy, money, and other valued currencies in a relationship, you need to think about the kinds of currency other people value. Once you understand *their* currency systems, your contributions will have more impact. The truth is that when you discover that others don't value your contributions, you will very likely feel resentment and disappointment. And too often you are also moved to say . . . **"After All I've Done for You."**

Why Equity Is Difficult to Manage

2. Trust Bankruptcy

Thrust ivrybody, but cut th' ca-ards.

MR. DOOLEY

Trust is critical in all of our relationships, with people at work, spouses, friends, and children. Several years ago researchers at North Carolina's Center for Creative Leadership identified the chief causes for executive failure in organizations. At the very top of their list were arrogance and insensitivity to other people. The next factor was **betrayal of trust**.

So on a scale of 1 to 10 (with 10 being the highest), how trustworthy are *you*? Most people tell us they are at least a 7 or an 8. Yet on that same scale, how trustworthy in general are *other* people? The typical responses we hear to this question are 4, 5, and 6. In fact, a recent survey by researchers at Boston University found that 80% of employees in organizations simply don't trust top management. Unfortunately, trust is an Outcome we expect *from* others in our relationships but an Input we are reluctant to provide *for* them. Why?

Trustworthy people tell the truth and keep their word. With this notion of trust in mind, make a quick mental list of occupations you perceive to be untrustworthy. Used car salespeople? Auto mechanics? Politicians? It's probably fairly easy for you to come up with even more. One reason we have trouble trusting others in relationships is our assumption that they will take advantage of us, lying, cheating, and stealing to get what they want from the relationship.

An executive headhunter once disclosed to us his most valuable interview question: "Would you lie?" He claims that a person who answers no is already lying. When the response is yes, he asks why and waits for job candidates to describe the circumstances in which they would not be honest. One CEO candidate answered, "Absolutely not!" When asked why not, the candidate said simply, "Because I have a bad memory!"

Another reason why trusting others is difficult is that trust in relationships does not come quickly. When beginning a new relationship, we tend to withhold trust until others prove that they can be trusted. New employees are less likely to be given access to confidential company information than are senior employees who have already justified our confidence in them. Before entering a marital relationship, we try to identify a pattern of trustworthy behavior in a potential spouse. Thus, we refuse to trust other people who say simply, "Trust me." Our position is, "Show me first that you can be trusted!"

Finally, we have problems trusting others because trust is fragile. Although developing a trusting relationship takes considerable time, destroying that trust doesn't take much at all. One simple violation of trust seems to prove that the other person in the relationship is not worthy of our future trust. Not wanting to appear naive and gullible, we therefore withhold it or give it grudgingly.

Because trust is an important Input *and* Outcome in relationships both at work and at home, it strongly influences perceptions of equity in relationships. Think about one of your relationships at work or off the job. Which of the following levels of trust characterizes that relationship?

- **Level 1: High Trust = Spontaneous Behavior**
  When a high level of trust exists, people show little concern about getting their share from the relationship. This is because they know that the other person will not take advantage of them. The mode of behavior at this level is for both parties to take from and give to the relationship spontaneously.
- **Level 2: Low Trust = Cautious Behavior**
  People in low-trust relationships are preoccupied with equity. The mode of behavior at this level is to get their fair share from the relationship, seeing to it that the other person gets no more than his or her fair share as well.
- **Level 3: Trust Bankruptcy = Aggressive Behavior**
  People in trust-bankrupt relationships seek to exploit the other person, withholding Inputs and trying to maximize Outcomes. The mode of behavior becomes "Get them before they get you. Who knows when they'll take advantage of you next?"

Think about your reactions when trust diminishes. You feel defensive and worry about being taken advantage of. Get them before they get you. While it's true that trust creates trust, distrust brings defensiveness and an "I win, you lose" relationship orientation. And when you've trusted someone else and they've disappointed you, your resentment and anger lead easily to the words . . .

"After All I've Done for You."

Why Equity Is Difficult to Manage

3. Hidden Expectations

Blessed is the man who expects nothing, for he shall never be disappointed.

ALEXANDER POPE

You might recognize this old riddle: A father and his son are driving to work one morning. A terrible accident takes place. The father is killed instantly and the son is badly injured. An ambulance rushes the son off to the hospital emergency room. He is taken quickly to surgery. The on-duty surgeon walks in, looks at the boy, and says, "I'm sorry. I can't operate on him. He's my son."

How can this be? The father was killed in the accident. You might guess that one father was a stepfather or perhaps a priest. Maybe the son was illegitimate or adopted. There are many possible explanations.

This simple riddle illustrates what we call hidden expectations, the third reason why equity in relationships is difficult to manage. These expectations are products of our past experiences as children, teenagers, and even adults. Perhaps your experiences tell you that all surgeons are male. And that's why you can't break through your own hidden expectations and determine that the surgeon in our riddle was actually the boy's mother.

We say these expectations are hidden for two reasons. First, people often don't realize how such expectations influence their own behavior. Second, even when they are aware of these expectations, too many people simply don't communicate them to others. Thus, hidden expectations lie dormant, influencing behavior in subtle ways, until some relevant event triggers them:

- A plant manager, raised during the Depression, is angry to discover that his younger-generation hourly employees don't want to work overtime. In his youth he would have been grateful for the opportunity.
- A new employee is troubled about the warning she received for arriving at work a few minutes past eight o'clock. In her previous job, people were allowed some flexibility in terms of when they reported to and left work.
- An executive, accustomed to the deference that subordinates show him, is surprised when his new secretary states that she doesn't fix coffee for anyone but herself.

A manufacturing executive recently told us about an incentive system his company installed after hearing repeated complaints from hourly employees about their wages. The system offered monetary bonuses for any employee who exceeded production quotas established by management. As soon as the incentive system was installed, productivity increased incredibly by almost 20%. Yet the executive was not pleased about the increased Outcomes that this system gave both management and labor. Instead, his attention was focused upon a set of hidden expectations he'd long had about people in organizations: "Now we *know* that people were goofing off for years before we began the incentives."

Hidden expectations often influence your treatment of people in organizations. Think back to the first person you ever supervised. You probably devoted considerable effort to this individual, carefully explaining your expectations, giving ample feedback about performance, and feeling genuinely responsible for his or her success at work. Yet over the years, as you began supervising more and more people, you might have become less communicative, perhaps expecting that these people had the same strengths as the first person you supervised. And when they didn't, you might have been surprised or even disappointed.

Too often people don't perform because we simply don't tell them what we want. Our expectations about their performance are hidden. In fact, studies in organizations show that people can't even summarize their job descriptions, let alone the more informal expectations their superiors have of them.

Hidden expectations abound in marriages as well—expectations about child-rearing, appropriate sexual behavior, budgeting money, relationships with friends and in-laws, and religious interests. Some people actually begin their marriage with the major hidden expectation of changing something about their spouse. They are often disappointed to learn that such change occurs neither easily nor quickly, if at all.

Thus, our past experiences—in jobs, marriages, and other relationships—build expectations about how people should behave. When we keep these expectations hidden, people aren't really sure what we expect from them. When they don't or simply can't conform to our expectations, we feel Under-Rewarded in the relationship. And sometimes we are moved to say . . .

"After All I've Done for You."

Why Equity Is Difficult to Manage

4. Stamp Collecting

It was the straw that broke the camel's back.

OLD CAMEL TRADER

You're probably familiar with the trading stamps that some people collect in grocery and department stores. They paste these stamps in little books, and when the books are filled, they redeem them for toasters, clocks, cars, even vacation trips. In relationships we collect and redeem stamps as well, but in less healthy ways.

The average marriage in this country lasts 6.8 years (perhaps you've heard of the seven-year itch). Some marriages follow a scenario like this: Think back to when you were newly married. Things usually go pretty well for at least the first two or three days. On the third morning of your brand-new relationship, you enter the bathroom and discover that your spouse has left the cap off the toothpaste tube. A white, sticky glob of toothpaste connects the tube to the porcelain sink. But instead of confronting your spouse, you say to yourself, "I'll let this slide. I love this person. This is the most important relationship in my life. Besides, the cap on the toothpaste tube is not that important." At the same time, however, you subconsciously paste a tiny stamp labeled "Toothpaste Tube Uncapped" into a small book in the back of your mind.

Several days later your spouse leaves the car unlocked while running an errand. Someone opens the car door and steals your tennis racket, the one that carried you to the club championship. Your spouse apologizes profusely, and you are quick to accept the apology. The relationship is simply too important. Nevertheless, you feel a bit like a martyr in overlooking your spouse's transgression. The "Stolen Tennis Racket" stamp finds its place in your small stamp collection.

Over the months and years your stamp collection grows: "Forgot Anniversary." "Criticized My Mother." "Insulted My Boss." "Overdrew Checking Account." Finally, roughly seven years down the road, your book is nearly filled with stamps, some smaller than others, but each evidence of your quiet suffering.

Then one day your spouse engages in a seemingly insignificant yet irritating behavior. And that behavior completes your book. You wake up one morning, look across the bed at your spouse, and state, "I want out of this relationship. I want a divorce." Astonished, your spouse asks why. So you throw the book at him or her. Better yet, you redeem each stamp individually, tearing it out of the book and hurling it righteously across the bedclothes: "Here's the toothpaste tube, here's my tennis racket, here's my birthday you forgot, here's the overdrawn checking account." And each stamp translates easily to, "After All I've Done for You."

We collect stamps in relationships by overlooking the other person's minor (and sometimes major) transgressions. Although we often feel better when we ignore behaviors that bother us, we lose track of very few of them. Each stamp is our Input to the relationship.

People in organizations collect stamps, too. A manager once told us about her collection on her boss. During the five years she worked for him, he did a lot of things to help complete her book. When they had lunch, he always seemed to be in the restroom when the check arrived. He let visitors park in her parking place at work. He took credit for her ideas and work. He by-passed her and dealt directly with her subordinates. He made jokes about women as managers. And he criticized his own boss and the company they worked for.

Then one day he falsified an expense form, claiming he'd taken a nonexistent trip. "I'd have probably turned him in anyway," she said. "But after all he'd done to me, I got a lot of satisfaction out of seeing him clean out his office after they fired him. I also got his job."

Why People Collect Stamps

The obvious alternative to stamp collecting is to confront others when they irritate or upset us. But we fail to do so for several reasons. First, we are inclined to give others what psychologists call **idiosyncratic credit**—credit that allows important people in our lives to behave in eccentric, idiosyncratic, and bothersome (to us) ways. Thus, we try to overlook their irritating behavior, telling ourselves that the relationship itself is more important. But as we collect stamps, their credit runs out.

In organizations, people collect stamps because they are victims of what is called the **Mum Effect**. Mum is an acronym that stands for **m**um about **u**ndesirable **mes**-sages. Few people enjoy being the bearer of bad news, especially subordinates. And the more promotable subordinates think they are, the more likely they are to withhold or distort negative information. The manager we just described to you was a victim of the Mum Effect. Of course, each time she chose not to speak up and confront her boss, she also added a stamp to her collection.

Finally, we often rationalize not confronting others because we're busy and don't want to take the time to call an annoying behavior to the other person's attention. And sometimes, especially when we've already accumulated a number of stamps, it's simply easier to avoid the strain of another confrontation.

Subtle Signs of Stamp Collecting

You can tell when other people are collecting stamps on you because they engage in behaviors we call **divorcements.** These are not relationship-ending behaviors such as quitting a job or actually filing for divorce. Instead, divorcements communicate in a subtle way, "I'm separating myself from this relationship." Employees begin habitually reporting to work late, taking extended breaks and lunch hours, and using up their sick days. Spouses leave the house in the middle of an argument or simply refuse to speak. Each divorcement is little more than an effort to remove the perceived inequity that increases with every stamp they collect.

Thus, people don't always end relationships over one major issue. Instead, they withdraw a little each day, counting their stamps and magnifying the significance of some of them. The event that creates their final stamp may or may not seem that important. But when the book is completed, they cash it in thinking . . .

"After All I've Done for You."

Thus, equity in relationships is difficult to manage because we often use the wrong psychological currency with others, because our relationship with them becomes trust-bankrupt, because both we and they are victimized by hidden expectations, and because both we and they engage in stamp collecting. And when any of these problems occurs, it really isn't difficult to feel the frustration and resentment of Under-Reward.

But we can manage these problems. In fact, we can reduce the chances that they'll occur, as well as combat them effectively if they do. In the next chapter, we'll explore everyday strategies for managing equity and getting more out of relationships.

4

Managing Equity to
Get the Results You Want
from Relationships

When a relationship isn't going well—when others
don't perform the way we want them to—we often tend
to feel a bit helpless. There's not much we can do. The
relationship is mostly out of our control. This is because
we also tend to focus too much on the *other person's* behavior. It's what the *other person* contributes to the relationship that we like or don't like. It's what the *other person*
does or does not do that helps or hurts the relationship.
Thus, we tend to feel that the world would be a better
place if everyone else did things more like we do them.

But as we begin this discussion of ways you can manage relationships more effectively, remember first that
many people at work and at home really do feel Under-
Rewarded. Recall also that this feeling of Under-Reward
is only a *perception* that they have. The facts might or
might not verify their perception, but *perceptions are all
that count in relationships.*

The reality is that in most relationships you have far
more control than you think you do. The reality is that in
most relationships:

- **You** have power over other people's **Inputs** to the relationship.
- **You** have power over other people's **perceptions** of their **Inputs** to the relationship.
- **You** have power over other people's **Outcomes** from the relationship.
- **You** have power over other people's **perceptions** of their **Outcomes** from the relationship.

Put simply, *you* have the power, the ability, to influence others' actual Inputs and Outcomes, as well as their perceptions of their Inputs and Outcomes in the relationship.

The influence you have comes from what we call the **Equity Power Paradigm.*** This paradigm gives you five ways—five powers you can use—to manage equity at work and at home—and get the results you want from relationships.

The Equity Power Paradigm

1. The Power of Perspective

I complained because I had no shoes—until I met a man who had no feet.

PERSIAN PROVERB

Perhaps you've read the poem about the six wise men who wanted to learn about elephants. So they visited one. But because they were all blind, they couldn't actually see

---

***Paradigm** (par-a-dime): a model or scheme that helps us organize and understand something better. We use the term here to describe an overall approach to managing relationships effectively.

the elephant. Therefore, each wise man touched a part of the elephant to determine what the animal was like. And each man drew a different conclusion:

- The first stumbled into the elephant's side and decided that an elephant is like a wall.
- The second touched the elephant's tusk. He compared the elephant to a spear.
- The third held the elephant's trunk and concluded that elephants are similar to snakes.
- The fourth felt the elephant's leg and decided that elephants are much like trees.
- The fifth, holding the elephant's ear, stated that elephants are very much like fans.
- The sixth, who grasped the elephant's tail, claimed that all elephants are like ropes.

The poem concludes . . .

> And so these men of Indostan,
> Disputed loud and long.
> Each in his own opinion,
> Exceeding stiff and strong.
> Though each was partly in the right,
> And all were in the wrong.

In relationships we sometimes behave like the six blind men who "saw" the world from different perspectives. As you already know, there are three faces of equity—your perception, the other person's, and the facts. And people often feel Under-Rewarded because they wear perceptual blinders. Like the blind men feeling the elephant, they become so locked into their own perceptions that they simply can't see or understand either your perceptions or the facts.

Differing perceptions of equity come from differing *perspectives* of Inputs and Outcomes in a relationship. You have the power both to *recognize* and to *change* the perspectives of others.

Recognizing Perspectives

When we introduced you to the Equity Factor earlier in this book, we told you that psychologists aren't really sure how people evaluate their Inputs and Outcomes. Some people compare what they give and get to what other people who are like them—coworkers, friends, people in similar jobs—appear to give and get. Others compare their Inputs and Outcomes to a standard that past relationships (previous jobs, marriages, and so on) have written into their minds. Still others compare what they give and get to what the other party in the relationship (supervisor, organization, spouse) appears to be giving and getting in return. What **is** clear is that people do make comparisons, and this is the perspective they use to decide if they are getting equity.

Some years ago the Georgia legislature voted to award college professors in the state university system a 3½% pay raise. This small pay increase followed several years of 10% raises. You can imagine the resentment of Under-Reward that we professors felt after all we'd done for the university, the state, and the general welfare of society. Note also the influence our past raises had on our perceptions of the current pay increase.

The reactions to this sense of Under-Reward were predictable. In fact, a few of our colleagues even quit their jobs and found work elsewhere. Yet just a few months after the raises were announced, we attended a national professional society meeting, where we discovered that many of our fellow professors from other states had received no pay raises at all. Some of them had actually taken pay cuts! Indeed, because of a weak economy, pay increases for professors were modest all across the nation.

We returned home from these meetings feeling a bit more equity in our relationship with the university and the legislature. Why? The pay increase had not changed by a penny. What had changed was our *perspective,* from focusing on raises in previous years to being grateful that, unlike many of our peers around the country, we'd received at least something for our efforts.

So what perspective do you use in evaluating your pay? Previous raises? Coworkers? Your efforts on the job? Your spouse's salary? Just as you might use one or even all of these perspectives to decide if you have pay equity, so also do other people use many perspectives to evaluate *all* their Inputs and Outcomes on the job and in relationships at home. There's a comparison operating somewhere, and it's not always the same comparison you'd make.

The Role of Listening

You can identify other people's perspectives by simply *listening* to them describe *why* they feel Under-Rewarded. A bank manager recently told us about her surprise when a subordinate complained that his new desk was too small. She explained to him that his desk was the same size as every other loan officer's desk and that it was newer than the desks of several other loan officers. "I know that," he responded. "But it's smaller than my secretary's. And I do more work than she does." The bank manager bought him a credenza to put behind his desk, and he seemed satisfied. She probably should have let him do his secretary's work for a few days instead.

Sometimes the mere act of listening affects the perspectives people take. Recall how little time we spend actually talking to one another. A major reason people feel inequity is that they also feel that no one knows what they really do, what they contribute to the relationship. What better way to change their perspective than simply to take the time to *listen*.

When people feel Under-Rewarded, it's because the perspective they've chosen makes them feel that way. We can't do anything about their perspective unless we know what it is. And the only way to recognize their perspective is to get them talking and to listen carefully to what they say.

Changing Perspectives

Once you're aware of the perspectives others have chosen, you also have the power to manage and change those perspectives. Some years ago a colleague gave us this letter from a college student to her parents:

Dear Mother and Dad,

Since I left for college I have been remiss in writing to you. I am really sorry for my thoughtlessness in not writing before. I will bring you up to date now, but before you read on, please sit down. You are not to read any further unless you are sitting down. Okay?

Well, then, I am getting along pretty well now. The skull fracture I got when I jumped out of the window of my dormitory when it caught fire shortly after my arrival here is pretty well healed. I spent only two weeks in the hospital, and now I can see almost normally and get those sick headaches only once a day.

Fortunately, the fire in the dormitory (and my jump) was witnessed by an attendant at the gas station near the dorm, and he was the one who called the fire department and the ambulance. He also visited me in the hospital, and since I had nowhere to live because of the burnt-out dormitory, he was kind enough to invite me to share his apartment with him. It's really just a basement room, but it's kind of cute.

He is a fine boy, and we have fallen deeply in love and are planning to get married. We haven't set the exact date yet, but it will be before my pregnancy begins to show. Yes, Mother and Dad, I am pregnant. I know how much you are looking forward to being grandparents, and I know you will welcome the baby and give it the same love and devotion and tender care you gave me when I was a child.

The reason for the delay in our marriage is that my boyfriend has a minor infection, which prevents us from passing our premarital blood tests, and I carelessly caught it from him. But I know that you will welcome him into our family with open arms. He is kind and, although not well educated, he is ambitious. Although he is of a different race and religion from ours, I know your often-expressed tolerance will not permit you to be bothered by that.

Now that I have brought you up to date, I want to tell you that there was no dormitory fire. I did not have a skull fracture. I was not in the hospital. I am not pregnant. I am not engaged. I am not infected, and there is no boyfriend in my life. However, I am getting a D in History and an F in Biology, and I wanted you to see these grades in their proper perspective.

Your loving daughter,
Susie

You might remember our earlier story about the prince and the magician. Obviously, the Susie who wrote this letter pulled back her sleeves and tried to work magic on her unsuspecting parents. Changing perspectives can be a powerful tool in managing equity. But her letter also illustrates the most important key to changing others' perspectives—**communication**.

Managerial Communication and Perceptions of Equity

Several years ago the management of a large multinational corporation made an interesting discovery in examining the results of their annual employee opinion survey. As part of their analysis of survey responses, they identified the ten corporate locations where employees were most *satisfied* in their jobs and most *committed* to the company. They also identified the bottom ten locations where employee satisfaction and commitment were the lowest in the corporation.

Their objective was simply to find out if there were any differences between the top ten and bottom ten locations. What they actually discovered had far greater implications for managing equity in the workplace.

When they compared survey responses for the top and bottom locations, they found that employees at the top ten locations had much more favorable perceptions of their pay than employees at the bottom ten, who felt that they were generally underpaid. But comparison of the *actual* salaries (the facts) of top and bottom location employees showed no differences in the pay they received.

The Impact of Two-way Communication

Intrigued by this finding, management then examined employees' responses to the other questions on the employee opinion survey. To their surprise, only *one* of nearly 150 other survey questions distinguished between the top and bottom locations. At the top locations, employees also had very favorable perceptions of *two-way communication with their immediate manager*. At the bottom locations, they did not.

That was it . . . two-way communication with managers was what influenced employees' perceptions of equity at the top ten and their perception of *in*equity at the bottom ten. Two-way communication is a *potentially* powerful tool to manage the perception of equity.

As managers we can have a lot of influence on employees' perceptions of their pay, their jobs, and the organization. We can exercise this same influence at home—as husbands and wives—through communication.

First, as we've said before, you can recognize others' perspectives by listening to them talk about their Inputs and Outcomes. Second, simply talking about why they feel Under-Rewarded can give others a sense of catharsis. Not everyone who complains about being Under-Rewarded wants an actual change in the situation; for some, the chance to blow off steam is an Outcome in itself. Be aware, though, that many employees who sit around and criticize the organization and everybody in it believe that the satisfaction of complaining is the *only* Outcome available to them. And that's where the second side of two-way communication comes into play.

Communicating to Change Perspectives

When responding to the perspectives you identify in other people, you might realize that they are, in fact, Under-Rewarded. In that case, the only way to restore equity is to increase the rewards they receive. But if they really aren't Under-Rewarded, then you can help them change perspectives. And you do this in two ways.

First, you can change their **perception of Inputs.** Employees who feel that their efforts aren't sufficiently recognized and rewarded might need to see their efforts differently. Some people need to see their efforts in light of:

- the efforts of other people
- their efforts on previous projects
- their own skills and abilities
- the actual results of their efforts
- the increased expectations that a recent promotion brought

Second, you can change their **perception of Outcomes.** Some people also need to see the recognition and rewards they receive in light of:

- the recognition and rewards others get
- the future Outcomes from current Under-Reward
- the recognition and rewards they received on previous projects
- the expectations others have for rewards and recognition

Put simply, you need to help others remove the blinders of limited perspective by suggesting other perspectives for them. That's the **power of perspective.**

The Equity Power Paradigm

2. The Power of Positive Expectations

Treat people as if they are what they ought to be, and you help them become capable of being.

GOETHE

In the late 1700s an Italian professor invented a cure for toothaches. It was simple and guaranteed to work for an entire year. Suffering patients were instructed to crush between their thumb and forefinger a worm . . . one whose Latin name was *Curculio antiodontaligious.* The worm's remains were then applied to the problem tooth. Suspicions of quackery soon arose, and a special commission was appointed to determine if the professor's toothache cure really worked. The commission investigated hundreds of toothache patients, and almost 70% of them confirmed that their toothaches had surrendered instantly to the power of the worm!

You might smile at this old story of mind over matter. But the professor's patients *expected* a cure, and that's what they got. As we'll show you, people who expect to succeed generally do. Those who think they will fail generally have their expectations confirmed, too. The second power you have to manage relationships more effectively is the **power of positive expectations**.

How Positive Expectations Work

The idea that your expectations can influence the behavior of others has existed for centuries. Perhaps you've heard of the Pygmalion Effect. The original Pygmalion was a mythological king who carved an ivory statue of the ideal woman. He named the statue Galatea. And because she was so lifelike and so beautiful, Pygmalion fell in love with her. His belief in Galatea caused Aphrodite, the goddess of love, to bring the statue to life.

George Bernard Shaw based his play *Pygmalion* on this myth. It is the story of a professor who tries to change a flower girl into a proper lady. The power our expectations have on the behavior of others is reflected in lines spoken by the play's main character, Eliza Doolittle:

> The difference between a lady and a flower girl is not how she behaves, but how she's treated. I shall always be a flower girl to Professor Higgins, because he always treats me as a flower girl and always will; but I know I can be a lady to you, because you always treat me as a lady, and always will.

The Pygmalion Effect is an example of what is also called the self-fulfilling prophecy, a powerful but simple principle: **If you think it's going to happen, then it will.**

A friend of ours once told us how the self-fulfilling prophecy helped him avoid seasickness. He had heard on a radio talk show that some doctors who go deep-sea fishing put a tiny Band-Aid behind their ear before setting off on a fishing expedition. This Band-Aid somehow affected the balancing mechanism in the inner ear, thus warding off seasickness.

A few months later our friend had a chance to go deep-sea fishing while on a family vacation. He and his father-in-law secured some Band-Aids from their hotel's kitchen. As an extra precaution, they placed a Band-Aid behind each ear before setting out to sea.

The Band-Aids worked miraculously. Our friend reported that despite the lurching boat and the sickness of many of their fellow passengers, he and his father-in-law fished all day, eating sandwiches, candy bars, and apples and feeling absolutely no effects of the rolling sea. They even cured the seasickness of a young newlywed on the boat by sharing their extra Band-Aids with her.

More than a year later our friend learned that some doctors do indeed wear Band-Aids behind their ears when deep-sea fishing—Band-Aids soaked in a prescription drug called scopolamine. This motion sickness drug is slowly released through the skin and into the bloodstream and actually combats seasickness. But our friend had managed to do the same thing with *ordinary* Band-Aids. If you think it will happen, then it will.

Creating positive expectations means you plant self-fulfilling prophecies for success in the minds of others. And a host of studies has shown clearly that creating these expectations has *profound* effects on the performance of other people, in organizations, in the classroom, and in everyday situations.

Why Positive Expectations Work

Positive expectations work for two reasons. First, they change perspectives because they combat the negative expectations that people carry around like baggage from one relationship to another: jobs in which they weren't treated fairly, marriages in which they were taken advantage of, and even classes in school in which they didn't perform well.

Positive expectations change a person's perspective from "I can't succeed" to "I will succeed." The second reason positive expectations work is that when you communicate these expectations to others, you are at the same time giving Outcomes—important Outcomes—to them. Let's explore both these reasons for a few minutes.

Combating Negative Expectations

First, let's establish that people do tend to carry negative expectations with them. Imagine that you're attending a banquet with ninety-nine other people. You've finished the meal, and the banquet is coming to a close. As the toastmaster completes his announcements, he says: "And now for a special surprise. When you entered the room tonight, we wrote each of your names down on a slip of paper. The box in front of me contains all one hundred names. I'm going to stir these names up and draw only one. The person whose name I draw will receive a $10,000 cash prize!" You now have two options:

• Stand up and move toward the podium. The toastmaster is sure to draw your name.
• Stay in your seat and think, It probably won't be me. My chances are only one in a hundred. I never win these things anyway.

If you're like most other people, you chose the second option. Realistically, your chances of winning *are* only one in one hundred. Realistically, you also have absolutely *no control* over whose name the toastmaster will pull from the box. Since you're now in such a realistic mood, let's change the situation slightly.

You are now a prisoner in some far-off land. In fact, there are one hundred prisoners in the room. It's about lunchtime, and the chief guard strolls into the room. He announces: "I've got some bad news for you. We have enough food for only ninety-nine people. So I've written each of your names down on a slip of paper. The names are in this box. I'm going to stir these names up and draw one out. If I draw your name, we're going to take you outside and shoot you." You now have two options:

- Stand up and walk to the door. He's sure to draw your name.
- Stay in your seat and think, It probably won't be me. My chances are only one in a hundred. I never win these things anyway.

The irony in this illustration is that the odds in both situations are identical—one in one hundred. The amount of control we have is the same—none. Yet most of us think we'll get the bullets, but not the bucks.

How you can change other people's perspectives was dramatically illustrated for us by a fellow professor. One of the first courses he took in graduate school was statistics, something that many graduate students fear as much as other people fear dentists. Our friend had done poorly in high school math. In college, he had taken only two math courses, one of them twice.

So he entered his statistics classroom that first day with an understandable perspective: "I'll never get through this stuff." As the class began, the statistics professor went over the course assignments. Then he walked to the blackboard, picked up a piece of chalk, and nearly covered the board with a long mathematical equation, our friend's first message from the alien world of statistics.

The professor turned to the class and instructed them in a somber voice to memorize and understand the equation. It would be on the final exam. But then the professor put down his chalk, smiled, and said, "I know a lot of you are worried about surviving this class. But if you can add, subtract, multiply, and divide, then you can do statistics." Our friend claims that he can still remember the sighs of relief (mostly his) that swept through the classroom. He also remembers that, as it turned out, there was much more to statistics than basic math. "But by the time I found that out," he said, "I was doing so well it just didn't make any difference."

The power of the positive expectations you build in others can and does combat the baggage of negative expectations they tend to carry around with them. You do have influence over the perspective they choose. But the positive expectations you create also provide much-needed Outcomes for others.

The Outcomes of Positive Expectations

Picture yourself and a friend having lunch one sunny afternoon. "I've got a tournament this Saturday," your friend says. "What kind of tournament?" you ask. "Horseshoes," your friend answers. "I'm the state champion horseshoe pitcher." "You're kidding," you say. "I didn't know you played horseshoes." "Yup. In fact, I'm heading out to practice right after lunch. Want to toss some with me?" "Sure," you respond. "But I haven't played horseshoes in years." "That's OK," your friend says. "We'll just play for fun." Delighted, you accompany your friend to the local horseshoe pit.

As you step out of his car, your friend opens the trunk

and pulls out a black leather briefcase. He lays the brief-case on the hood of the car and opens it. There before you lie two chrome-plated horseshoes. And each one is en-graved at the top with your friend's initials.

He unpacks the horseshoes and together you walk over to the pit. Your friend takes two warm-up tosses, both ringers. He retrieves the shoes, and hands them to you. "Ready?" he asks. "I guess so," you answer hesitantly. "But it looks a lot tougher than I remember it was." "You're right," your friend says. "It *is* tough. And just looking at you, I'm not sure you're coordinated enough to pitch very well, anyway."

Some friend. Of course, a few of us will respond to this challenge by trying to prove our friend wrong. But real-istically, most of us are thinking, "What in the world am I doing here?"

So let's start over. Assume now that your friend has taken his two warm-up tosses and handed you the shoes. "Ready?" he asks. "I guess so," you answer hesitantly. "But it looks a lot tougher than I remember it was." "You're right," your friend says. "It *is* tough. But just looking at you, I think you'll turn out to be one dynamite horseshoe pitcher."

"One dynamite horseshoe pitcher." Think about the Outcomes your friend has given you in a simple phrase. Check those Outcomes against the Outcomes of Positive Expectations list on the opposite page.

When you communicate positive expectations to oth-ers, you give them Outcomes *before* they even attempt to perform—Outcomes that they would otherwise not have had. In doing so, you increase their sense of equity.

We began this discussion of positive expectations with a quote from the German philosopher Goethe: "Treat people as if they are what they ought to be, and you help

---

Outcomes of Positive Expectations

1. A sense of competence
2. A feeling of personal worth
3. Status
4. Belonging
5. A sense of confidence
6. A feeling of control

---

them become capable of being." Goethe's words also appear in the annual report of a Maryland firm that was recently recognized as one of the 100 best companies to work for in America. The words capture the power of positive expectations in building self-fulfilling prophecies for success in other people.

If you have children, you might have already used this power without realizing it. *Not* counting only children:

- Of the original 23 astronauts in the U.S. space program, 21 were first-born children. *All* of the original Mercury astronauts were first-borns.
- More than 50% of all U.S. presidents have been first-born children.
- More than 60% of people listed in *Who's Who in America* are first-born children.
- Nearly 50% of all members of the U.S. Congress are first-born children.

Statisticians tell us to expect that only about 33% of people in each of the above categories will be first-borns. Yet first-borns keep succeeding, much to the envy of those of us who have a different birth order.

For a time, some people (mostly first-borns) claimed

that the remarkable record of first-born success proved the genetic superiority of the first child in the family. But we think you'll find that their success is more a function of expectations than inheritance. With your first child, the tendency is to communicate expectations for success through all the attention and time the child receives. Later children sometimes don't receive these same expectations and the Outcomes that accompany them.

You can verify these expectations by checking the size of baby albums in your own family. If you're a first-born, then your baby album is probably bulging with pictures from your early life—in the nursery, arriving home, your first birthday, your first teddy bear, your first step, and numerous other firsts that first-borns lay claim to. If you're a second child, then your album is probably smaller. A third child, even smaller. And if you're the unfortunate fifth or sixth child in your family, then your baby album may well be one or two snapshots thrown in the back of some dresser drawer.

Positive expectations *work*. They help people overcome the baggage of negative expectations that they bring from previous relationships in which things didn't go well. They provide Outcomes that contribute to a sense of equity in a relationship. They replace those hidden expectations that make equity difficult to manage with clear expectations for performance.

You can use the power of positive expectations in many situations at work—with new employees in their first day on the job, people who are trying to accomplish difficult tasks, transfers into a new position, or people who simply need the psychological lift that positive expectations provide. At home your positive expectations can build self-fulfilling prophecies for success as your spouse enters a new job or as one of your children takes new classes in school. Find a way of saying to them, "Just looking at you, I think you'll turn out to be one dynamite horseshoe pitcher."

Finally, by themselves positive expectations are powerful incentives to perform well. Yet they can't *guarantee* performance. If you build positive expectations in others who nevertheless fail, then they'll likely blame themselves and you for their failure—one more entry for the stamp collection. The only thing worse than not having positive expectations is to have them but fail anyway. So let's explore some other components of the **Equity Power Paradigm,** some ways to keep others' expectations positive by guaranteeing success.

The Equity Power Paradigm

3. The Power of Goal-setting

If you don't have goals, then there's nothing to shoot for.

ANONYMOUS

Each day across this country many people drag into work in the morning. They plod through the day, doing only what they need to do to keep up. At quitting time, they rush out to the parking lot, leap into their cars, and launch themselves like guided missiles, *away* from work.

Where are these suddenly energized people going? Most of them are simply headed toward some activity that gives them something to shoot for—golf, tennis, gardening, bowling, hunting, fishing, running, jogging, crossword puzzles, softball, baseball, and computer games.

How long would people watch football if we removed the goal posts and yard lines? How long would we play golf if we didn't keep score? How often would you garden if nothing ever grew? We enjoy these activities because they give us something to shoot for. And we seem to do a far better job of establishing goals in our recreational activities than we do in relationships.

Literally hundreds of studies have shown what you probably already know: people with goals perform better. So why aren't people in organizations performing any better than they are? Why do nearly 85% of them say that they could perform better on the job if they wanted to? It's not that we don't know that goal-setting works. Instead, it's *how* we set those goals that gives us the power to manage equity in relationships. In fact, you can set goals in one of three ways. We'll help you decide which way is best.

"Do Your Best" Goal-setting: Why It Doesn't Work

"Do your best" is one of the most common ways we set goals for people in organizations. Using this type of goal-setting, we set general goals for others: "Just do your best." You'd think that asking for someone's best would be enough to guarantee performance. But it isn't. And if you'll think about the activities you enjoy *off* the job, then you'll understand why.

We asked a golfing friend what his handicap was. "My swing," he answered. Actually, he has a 15 handicap. And he's working hard to get it to 10. Other golfers are trying simply to break 100 (or maybe 150).

Ask tennis players what their goal is during a match. Besides getting serves in and clearing the net, most will say, "To win!" Hunters want to bag the limit. Runners work to improve their times. Across this country, family rooms, recreation rooms, bedrooms, and sometimes garages are cluttered with trophies and other mementos of individual and group exploits in goal achievement.

So think for a few minutes about *why* you enjoy those off-the-job activities. And check your reasons against the list of Outcomes of *specific* goals you see below. If you play golf, there's the *challenge* of trying to break 100, or to hit every green in regulation, or to shoot par. And the goal also brings many *problems to solve,* such as getting out of the woods or a sandtrap. Tennis players enjoy *competition* with others, and the game calls for their best athletic *abilities*. Runners feel personally *responsible* for improving their times and *make decisions* about how fast or slow to run at different points in a race. The *Outcomes* from goal-setting cause our performance to improve.

Like the Outcomes of positive expectations, people receive the Outcomes of *specific* goals even before they per-

---

Outcomes of Setting Specific Goals

1. Challenge
2. Problems to solve
3. Competition with self or others
4. Making use of one's abilities
6. Making decisions

form. And these Outcomes drive their desire and direct their efforts to succeed. Specific goals give them something to shoot for.

In organizations specific goals function the same way. Try telling someone who works for you to "Just do your best." When they produce only 75% of what you expected, you'll be disappointed. And you'll be even more disappointed the next time out, when they produce 75% of the 75% they produced the first time.

Forget "Do Your Best" goal-setting. Despite the fact that it's the easiest way to set goals (that's probably why we set them this way), it perpetuates those hidden expectations that make relationships difficult to manage. "Do Your Best" doesn't tell people what you really expect. Nor does "Do Your Best" goal-setting provide any Outcomes for others—Outcomes that will help them develop a better sense of equity in your relationship with them.

Assigned Goal-setting: Why It Doesn't Always Work

Using this second approach to goal-setting, you set *specific* goals for others. Assigning specific goals clearly gives people something to shoot for. The only problem is how high (or low) the goals should be.

When we set goals for ourselves—saving $10,000 for investments, losing twenty pounds, paying off our credit cards—we're in a good position to set these goals, because we also know whether or not we can reach them. Thus, we make the goals challenging but attainable. However, when we set goals for others, we don't always have enough information to know how high or low the goals should be.

To understand better the problem of setting specific goals for others, take a ten-minute break and try this exercise: Get out a blank sheet of paper. At the top of the page write "RHODE ISLAND." Your goal is to make a list of thirty words out of any combination of letters in this state's name. You have only ten minutes to finish the job, so work quickly.

How'd you do? We hope you got to thirty, because almost everyone does. And when you do, you receive the Outcomes of achieving specific goals listed below. Note that a sense of accomplishment, the most important Outcome that people want from their jobs, is at the top of that list.

Outcomes of Achieving Specific Goals

1. Sense of accomplishment
2. Feelings of personal worth
3. Status
4. Sense of competence
5. Pride
6. Achievement

We've also discovered that some people get to thirty words in less than four minutes. And then they *quit working*. If we'd set your goal at forty, then you'd have likely made that goal, too. And that's a 33% increase in production. Perhaps you can see the results of setting goals too low.

Setting goals too high, however, can result in frustration and in people giving up. When using this exercise in our classes and training programs, we've sometimes told people that their goal is sixty words. One person out of about forty will reach this goal. Others will stop at fifteen or twenty. They realize quickly that they can't make goal and they give up. And none of those critical Outcomes of achieving specific goals is available to them.

A university president once told us how her father used high goals to ensure her success as a child in grammar school. She still remembers greeting him at the front door when he came home from work one evening. In her small hands she held the results of a spelling test. "See, Father, I made a ninety-eight," she said. Her father looked at her grade, paused, and then asked, "So who made the hundred?"

Her father's strategy is not lost on American managers. During a recent recession one department store chain set out to improve its sales through a goal-setting program. When commissioned salespeople opened their weekly pay envelopes, they found computerized notes attached to their paychecks. Here's a sample: "During your last pay period, you produced $7,000 in sales. Your quota for the next pay period is $10,500."

At first the sales force responded to the challenge of this 50%-per-pay-period increase in sales. And sales did climb. But about four weeks into the program, the salespeople realized that their goals were and would always be impossible to reach. Under enormous pressure from a resentful and disenchanted sales force, management discontinued the goal-setting program. Sales immediately dropped to pre-program levels. What's worse is that the sales force will view any future attempts at goal-setting as little more than management manipulation.

Thus, assigned goal-setting provides a target—something to shoot for. If you know what people are capable of achieving, then assigning goals should work. Perhaps you're familiar with IBM's 100% Club. Membership in the club is limited to IBM salespeople who have made 100% of their quota for the preceding year. Interestingly enough, nearly 80% of the IBM sales force belongs to the club. That's because management has set challenging yet attainable goals. And 80% of IBM's sales force is meeting quota, joining the club, and collecting a host of relationship Outcomes that goal-setting offers.

But if you aren't sure what people are capable of, then you might set the goals too high, creating a sense of resentment in some Under-Rewarded people. Or you might set them too low, giving Outcomes to others at the expense of lost performance and productivity. If either of these dangers exists, then you'll be much better off, especially in relationships at home, to use the third form of goal-setting—participation.

Participative Goal-setting: Why It Works

Participative goal-setting means that you allow people to help set goals for themselves; they *participate* in the process. Participative goal-setting ensures that goals are *realistic*—that people who work hard can attain them. It has two other advantages as well.

First, people who set goals for themselves often set *higher* goals than the goals you would have assigned to them. An important exception is people who feel severely Under-Rewarded. They'll tend to set goals low enough to put you out of business.

Second, people who set goals for themselves will work

harder to reach them. That's because they *own* the goals. And because the goals belong to them (not you), they'll be much more committed to making sure goals are met.

Participative goal-setting doesn't involve turning people loose to set and reach goals on their own. Instead, you talk to them, help them choose their goals, agree on what they can do, and let ownership and commitment do the rest.

We've already listed twelve psychologically important Outcomes that specific and realistic goals can provide. If you use participative goal-setting, then you are also giving one additional Outcome to others—*trust* in their ability to help manage themselves and their relationship with you. So give them something to shoot for. But let them help pick the target.

Goal-setting, then, results in agreed-upon performance expectations. Because of the many Outcomes that specific, realistic, and participative goals provide, goal-setting gives you the power to manage equity better in relationships at work and at home. Goal-setting also forces you to confront those hidden expectations for how others should perform. Whether it's an employee who is working to cut errors by 10% or a spouse trying to stay within budget, goal-setting brings your expectations into the open.

Finally, remember that you can use goal-setting on a daily basis. The next time someone asks you when you need a report finished, don't say "any time next week." Instead, ask that person when it can be finished. And agree that five o'clock on Tuesday will be just fine.

The Equity Power Paradigm

4. The Power of Performance Feedback

When someone does something well, applaud.
You'll make two people happy.

SAMUEL GOLDWYN

It was his first circus. His grandfather had promised to take him on his next birthday. And now here they were. The young boy was mystified by the daring feats of the circus animals—elephants that knelt down, rolled over like dogs, and stood majestically on their hind legs; horses that trotted in line around the ring, allowing their riders to stand on their backs and jump off and on at will. But the boy was most amazed by a huge male lion that leaped effortlessly about the caged ring, climbed a ladder, crept along a narrow board nearly fifteen feet in the air, and then jumped through a large, flaming hoop.

"Grandpa, how do they get that lion to do that?" "Do what, son?" "How do they get that lion to jump through that hoop when it's on fire?"

The old man smiled. "Well, it's like this. They go out into the jungle, set a hoop on fire, hang it from a tree, and wait. They capture the first lion that jumps through the hoop and bring it back to the circus."

"Is that really how they do it?" the boy asked in disbelief. "Not really," the grandfather answered. "What they really do is go out into the jungle and look for a lion, preferably a young one. They catch him, bring him back to the circus, and begin to train him.

"When they begin training the lion, they hang the hoop

at ground level. It's not on fire because lions are afraid of fire. They watch the lion walk around the ring. Sooner or later he walks through the hoop. As soon as he does, they give him some meat to eat. When he walks through it again, they give him more meat. Pretty soon the lion realizes that if he walks through the hoop, he'll have lunch.

"The only problem is that watching a lion stroll through a hoop doesn't excite many circusgoers. So bit by bit they raise the hoop. And each time the lion jumps through, he gets a reward. Sooner or later the hoop is fifteen feet in the air. Now, most lions can't jump that high. So that's why the lion is willing to climb the ladder and creep along the board to get to the hoop.

"But even seeing a lion jump through a hoop fifteen feet in the air isn't that exciting to some people. So they set the hoop on fire. Of course, lions don't like fire. But they do like fresh meat. So the lion jumps through the flaming hoop, gets even more meat, and finds out that this is an easy way to go hunting."

"But Grandpa, why does the lion tamer keep cracking his whip like that?" the boy asked. The old man chuckled. "It's just for show, my boy. The lion could care less, and his master knows it."

You're probably not a lion tamer, although you might sometimes feel like one when you try to manage relationships. But our story has two morals:

- **People perform better in relationships when they get feedback on performance.**
- **People perform better in relationships when the feedback they get is positive.**

Think again about the activities you enjoy off the job. One reason you enjoy these activities is that they give you something to shoot for. Most of them also give you feedback about your performance. You *see* what happens when you hit a golf ball or serve a tennis ball. You *watch* your garden grow. You *hear* the sound of your favorite musical instrument when you play it.

But at work we often don't get this feedback from the job itself. Instead, we have to wait until someone tells us how we're doing. And too often we think the wait will last forever—unless the feedback is negative.

In organizations we manage by exception: "If you *don't* hear from me, that means you're doing OK. But make a mistake, and I'll climb down your throat." Thus, we crack the whip, but it's not for show. When was the last time you called a meeting with the sole purpose of praising someone who had done something *right*? When was the last time you sat down with your spouse with the sole purpose of listing the things he or she does *well* in your relationship?

Negative feedback is punishment that reduces the motivation to perform in relationships. Sometimes, however, we need to use negative feedback when no alternative seems to exist. In fact, you'll see some suggestions for giving negative feedback later in this chapter.

But if you emphasize positive feedback, then you'll be

Outcomes of Positive Feedback

1. Recognition
2. Feelings of competence
3. Sense of accomplishment
4. Status
5. Appreciation from others
6. Feelings of achievement
7. Personal worth

surprised at how rarely you need to resort to negative approaches to relationship management. Because when you give positive feedback, you also give much-needed Outcomes that build equity in the relationship. And from this sense of equity comes better performance.

Qualities of Effective Positive Feedback

If you believe in the power of positive feedback, then you'll probably recognize the four qualities that make positive feedback effective.

I. Feedback Should Be Immediate: When you hit a golf ball, you know almost immediately how far down the fairway (or into the woods) it's going to travel. In tennis the ball is either in or out. And when you bowl, you actually see the pins fall.

Unfortunately, the only feedback some people get at work is at performance review time—once a year, once every six months, or perhaps once every three months. One company actually schedules these ego-threatening events on the employee's birthday! And it's interesting that in one of this nation's most cherished institutions— marriage—no established mechanism for feedback even exists.

Many jobs that people perform in organizations don't in themselves give the immediate feedback that we get when playing golf or tennis. So your job as a relationship manager is to provide frequent feedback, especially on employee contributions that don't give immediate feedback themselves.

In fact, feedback is the central theme in a host of training programs conducted for managers in organizations, teachers in schools, and partners in marriage. But we sometimes wonder how useful all this training is.

For example, nearly fifteen years ago we developed a survey to evaluate communication between managers and their subordinates. Consider the following statement that managers find on the survey:

I LET MY SUBORDINATES KNOW WHEN
THEY'RE DOING A GOOD JOB

Now pick an option that shows how often you as a manager do this:

Always   Frequently   Occasionally   Seldom   Never

If you chose Always or Frequently, then your answer is like that of over 3,000 managers we've surveyed in organizations throughout the U.S. In fact, on a scale of 1 to 5 (1 = never; 5 = always), the average response for all those managers is 4.3. So it looks as if everyone is doing pretty well.

But let's look at a statement we presented to subordinates about how often they *received* feedback from those same 3,000 managers:

MY SUPERVISOR LETS ME KNOW
WHEN I'M DOING A GOOD JOB

Choose one of the five options to show how often your own supervisor or manager gives you positive feedback. If you're like nearly 11,000 people at *all* levels of organizations who've responded to our survey, then you probably didn't choose Always or Frequently. On the same 1 to 5 scale, the average score is only 2.3! We call this the **Feedback Gap**—4.3 (for the managers) versus 2.3 (for the subordinates).

The Feedback Gap

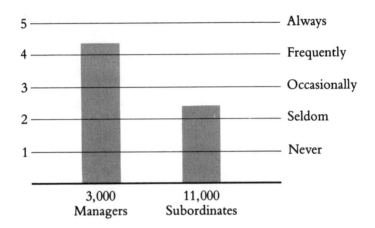

The Feedback Gap: A 200% difference between the amount of positive feedback managers say they *give* and the amount of positive feedback subordinates say they *get*

With a 200% difference between 3,000 managers who say they give feedback and 11,000 subordinates who say they don't receive it, you're probably wondering who's right. But it isn't a matter of who's right and who's wrong. Recall the three faces of equity.

The facts would probably tell us that the real feedback score is somewhere between 2.3 and 4.3. But the face of equity that really counts in terms of how people perform is the one that produced the 2.3 score!

So, in your important relationships at work and at home, you need to realize that the other person probably has a much lower perception of the immediacy of your feedback than you do. People don't want to wait until the game is over to find out how well they did. That's why we have scoreboards in football stadiums and scoresheets in bowling alleys. If you want to manage relationships with others more effectively, then catch them in the act of doing something right. And tell them so. Right away.

2. Feedback Should Be Specific: A second quality of the feedback you get from activities you enjoy is that it's *specific*. The feedback tells you exactly how you did. In bowling, you see how many pins you knocked over. In golf, you see how far you hit the ball. But in relationships, if you receive any positive feedback at all, it tends to be fairly general: "You're doing a fine job." "Thanks for the good work." "I like being married to you."

This is not to say you shouldn't pay general compliments to other people. But *specific* statements provide the Outcomes just as *general* statements do. And they reinforce the *specific* kinds of behaviors in which you want others to engage. If you reward people's behaviors, then they'll tend to repeat them: "Thanks for getting this agenda done so quickly." "I'm impressed by how well you organize your thoughts on paper." "It's great to have someone I can count on when things get tough."

People want to be part of relationships. That's why they are joiners from the time they are children, becoming members of clubs in high school, civic and professional organizations, sports teams, and social groups. Their need to belong may also be reflected in the fact that nearly 85% of people who divorce for the first time remarry within five years.

But people also want to be recognized for their *unique* contributions to relationships. They want to stand out.

That's why organizations have employees of the month, million-dollar round tables, and 100% clubs. Specific feedback recognizes the unique Inputs that people give to your relationship with them.

3. Feedback Should Be Tied to Performance: Effective feedback is immediate and specific. It is also tied directly to performance. Some years ago a consulting firm marketed a special wrist watch. This watch had nine stems, one regular stem plus eight dummies. The dummy stems were painted red, and all you could do was either pull them out or push them in.

Your job was to wear this watch to work in the morning, pulling all eight dummy stems out. Then, between eight and nine o'clock, you'd approach one of your subordinates and say, "You're doing great work for us around here. We really appreciate you."

You would then walk away, punching one stem in. Between nine and ten o'clock you'd repeat this ritual with a second subordinate. Between ten and eleven you'd visit a third subordinate. By day's end, you'd have given out eight strokes, timed perfectly by the red reminders on your wrist.

The watch is helpful because it reminds you to give feedback. Many of us desperately need that reminder. But notice that the feedback is based upon timed intervals, not performance. Positive feedback works when you tie it to something the person has done. And you don't want to reward people who aren't performing.

4. Feedback Should Be Genuine: You might also think that the watches aren't genuine, that they're a gimmick. A lot of gimmicks work. That's why advertising sells products. But when an employee asks what those red things are on your watch, you can't very well say that your watch has the measles. The final quality of effective positive feedback is that it's *genuine.*

Almost all of us want others to perceive us as genuine. That may be one reason why we don't give any more positive feedback than we do. Will they believe us? From the time we're children, we learn to pay compliments to others: "Gosh, Granny, I like your dress." "That's a good-looking tie, Harry." Yet you might feel terribly awkward when, as an adult supervising others, you catch them doing something right.

But think for a few moments about how easily you empathize with professional actors and actresses, how utterly believable they are in the roles they play. The reason they're believable is *practice.* They've either rehearsed the part repeatedly or played it so many times that making us feel sympathy, support, dislike, or fear comes naturally. So if you want to become a genuine giver of positive feedback, then simply do it over and over until you get the part right. Lots of people are waiting for your performance.

Thus, positive feedback works when you give it right away, when you make it specific, when you tie it to performance, and when it's genuine. Such feedback is powerful because it gives important Outcomes to others. With these Outcomes comes equity. And people who have equity perform better in relationships.

The Dilemma of Giving Negative Feedback

As we mentioned earlier, you sometimes have no option but to give others negative feedback. While a strong case can be made for not doing so, it's also true that you'll occasionally need to correct undesirable behaviors.

Some years ago management expert Douglas McGregor outlined what he called the Hot Stove principles of punishment. We've adapted McGregor's principles here to provide you with five guidelines for giving negative feedback.

Guideline 1: If you touch a hot stove, you get burned right away. In human relationships our reaction to undesirable behavior is not always immediate. Many of us wait days before we tell others we're unhappy about what they did. Sometimes we wait so long that the other person doesn't have a clear idea what the punishment is for.

Effective positive feedback is immediate. So is effective negative feedback. If you need to give negative feedback, do it right away.

Guideline 2: The hot stove's punishment is intense the very first time you touch it. In human relationships we tend to give negative feedback fairly gently the first time. Later, we see the undesirable behavior repeated, so we administer a larger dose of punishment. If the behavior occurs again, we use even stronger punishment. Yet if your negative feedback, like that of the hot stove, is fairly intense the first time, then you'll have less need to use it in the future.

Guideline 3: The hot stove punishes only the hand that touched it. In human relationships we tend to get personally involved when giving negative feedback and sometimes lose our tempers in doing so. Thus, instead of punishing a single behavior, like the hot stove does, we punish the entire person.

Your goal in giving negative feedback is to change a behavior, not an entire personality. If you maintain your objectivity and focus only on the behavior you want to change, then your feedback will be more effective.

Guideline 4: The hot stove is universally consistent. No matter who touches it, the result is always the same. In human relationships we sometimes punish one person for a specific behavior, but not other people who engage in the same behavior. This kind of inconsistency makes others wonder either what we want or who our favorites are. Your reaction, like the hot stove's, should be consistent, no matter who engages in the behavior.

Guideline 5: If you touch a hot stove, you have ways to stop the pain. In human relationships we sometimes punish others without letting them know what acceptable behavior is in that situation. We get so caught up in punishing what we don't like that we fail to let others know what is desirable. What alternative do they have? For negative feedback to be effective, you need to tell others what they should or shouldn't do to stop the pain of punishment.

If you'll think through these five guidelines the next time you need to give negative feedback, then you'll have a better chance of changing the behavior before it becomes a major relationship issue.

But try to emphasize the positive. Positive feedback can help you avoid situations in which you feel a need to say negative things to others. People want to know when they're doing something right, but too often we don't tell them.

A Different Kind of Hunger

Estimates are that between 1.5 and 15 million people in the United States go to sleep hungry every night. It's a real tragedy, especially because we've spent literally billions of dollars to combat hunger in this country. But as we conclude this section on giving feedback, we'll remind you that there are probably important people in your life relationships who also go to sleep hungry every night— hungry for just a little recognition.

So the next time one of your employees does a good job, say so right away. When your spouse does something that you really appreciate, say so right away. When one of your children does something that makes you proud, say so right away. And count on the fact that the Outcomes you give through positive feedback build equity in the relationship and make you a much better relationship manager.

The Equity Power Paradigm

5. The Power of Novel, Rewarding Behaviors

> But mount to paradise by the stairway of surprise.
>
> RALPH WALDO EMERSON

Relationships have many rewarding rituals. In some organizations, employees get service awards. They might receive a five-year pin and get an emerald for the pin after ten years. During the next twenty years, diamonds find their way onto the pin as well. In marriages we celebrate anniversaries, the silver twenty-fifth, the golden fiftieth, and the diamond sixtieth. And almost all of us eat birthday cake to celebrate the passing of one more year.

These rituals, rewarding as you might think, are based upon a single factor—survival. Survive the job, survive the marriage, survive yourself, and another reward comes your way.

We don't mean to criticize the time-honored traditions that our society values. But too many relationships are inhabited by *survivors,* not *winners.* Too many people never even get a taste of what it's like to be a winner. And that's the **power of novel, rewarding behaviors**—to make winners out of survivors.

Some years ago an executive we know was appointed president of a large commercial construction firm. When he took control of the company, it was near bankruptcy. One of his first acts as company president was to sign a contract with a large corporation to build an office building in thirteen months at a price of $23 million.

When he signed the contract, he knew he couldn't complete the job in thirteen months. Nor could he do it for $23 million. But he needed the business, so he took his chances. Actually, he did a lot more than that.

Late one evening he visited the construction site to check on the building's progress. The foundation for the building was being set, and he noticed something interesting. Some workers had laid cement blocks, the components of the foundation, nearly eight feet high. Other workers across the construction site had managed only three or four feet of progress on their cement walls. Clearly, some people were performing extremely well. Others were doing only marginal or, at best, average work.

The president walked to his car, took out some envelopes and paper, and returned to the construction site. As he passed the areas where people had met or exceeded his expectations for performance, he stopped and wrote a note that said simply, "Thanks for a great job." He then took a twenty-dollar bill from his wallet, wrapped it inside the note, put the note and the money in the envelope, and left it there. That night he spent almost $400 of his personal money. But in his words, "You should have seen people laying cement blocks the next day!"

The president rewarded both quality and quantity of employee performance in other ways: catered luncheons, T-shirts, decals for hard hats, more cash bonuses, and on-the-spot pay raises for exceptional work. In total, he spent nearly $48,000 on novel, rewarding behaviors during the building's construction. But his employees finished the building two months *early* and at almost $100,000 *under* the contract price.

Today this executive is still president of that construction firm. He's also its owner. And when he negotiates contracts for office buildings, he insists that the contract price include money for his novel, rewarding behaviors program. In return, he can ensure buyers that a quality building will be completed at price and by the deadline. He's a genuine winner. But his employees are winners, too.

Novel, rewarding behaviors (NRBs for short) are the unexpected but pleasant things you do in relationships to show others that you recognize and appreciate their performance. NRBs give important Outcomes to others.

NRBs at Work

Unlike our executive friend, you don't need to spend thousands of dollars to begin a program of NRBs. Of course, in his case $48,000 was a small investment for the return he received. But here are some examples of

> ### *Outcomes of Novel, Rewarding Behaviors*
>
> 1. Unique recognition
> 2. Variety in the relationship
> 3. Surprise
> 4. Sense of accomplishment
> 5. Sense of belonging
> 6. Status
> 7. Personal worth
> 8. Appreciation from others

NRBs that have made spontaneous winners out of survivors:

- personal visits at work from top executives to employees who excel
- afternoons or days off
- trophies, wall plaques, gold or silver pins that are awarded for exceptional performance
- letters to employees' spouses commending the employees' performance
- personal notes of thanks written on paychecks
- managers treating performers to lunch
- birthday cards signed by the CEO and sent to employees' homes
- achievement decals for hard hats, badges for uniforms, and T-shirts
- small cash awards with personal thank-you
- notes inside employees' desk or calendar
- telephone calls at home from top executives to employees who excel

This list is hardly exhaustive. But maybe it prompts you to think about the unusual but rewarding things you can do in relationships at work.

We have several kinds of NRBs in our department at the university. One of them is the Phi Beta Krappa award. Begun many years ago, the award recognizes those who do the eccentric, sometimes absent-minded things that college professors are known for. The award itself is an orange plastic bedpan with the words PHI BETA KRAPPA inscribed on it with blue plastic tape.

One recent recipient earned the award for throwing a library book into the trash; he claimed the book itself was trash. The unhappy library personnel called our department head, seeking thirty dollars to replace the book. At the awards ceremony (a special department meeting), the keeper of the award entered the room dressed in full academic regalia. In one hand he carried a lighted candle (signifying what we college professors call the "search for truth"). In the other hand was the bedpan.

After briefly describing what the nominee had done to qualify for the award, the presentation was made. The recipient engaged in a ritualistic denial of his behavior, there was applause, and the meeting ended.

Both of us try hard not to become Phi Beta Krappa award nominees, especially because recipients are required to hang the award prominently in their office until someone else earns it. But we also recognize that the award is just another way of saying to people: "Sure, you screwed up. But you belong here. And we're glad to have you as part of our group."

NRBs at Home

You can also use NRBs to manage relationships off the job. They provide the same Outcomes as NRBs at work, but they are often much more meaningful.

A friend once told us about a significant NRB in his marriage. He'd been having a rough time at work, too much traveling, too much stress, and not enough time off. He came home from a business trip one Friday evening and began talking to his wife about his problems at work. They discussed his career nearly the entire weekend. Despite his wife's support and encouragement, he didn't feel much better when he drove to the airport that Sunday afternoon.

He flew into Chicago and checked into a hotel there, feeling tired and lonely and not looking forward to the next morning's business meeting. In the hotel room he hung his suits in the closet and stuffed the rest of his clothes into a dresser drawer. Then he carried his shaving kit into the bathroom and opened it up. There, lying on top of his toothpaste tube, was a handwritten note from his wife: "I love you!"

In addition to those Outcomes we listed for you earlier, NRBs can sometimes give others a much-needed psychological lift and further cement the bonds in your relationship.

As at work, there are countless ways you can engage in novel, rewarding behaviors in off-the-job relationships, including small gifts for "unspecial" occasions. Another executive described a coupon book her husband gave her. Inside the book were coupons for back rubs, foot massages, and the like. He'd even included some blank coupons for her to fill out as she liked and redeem whenever she wanted to—much better, we think you'd agree, than redeeming a collection of relationship stamps!

So the next time you're going out of town, leave a special note between the sheets so that someone important to you will find it when climbing into the empty bed.

A Word of Caution

At work and at home, NRBs can help everyday survivors of relationships experience the feeling of being winners. But two final cautions as you think about ways to use NRBs: First, be sure that you're engaging in the right psychological currency. Not every employee will appreciate a T-shirt, a decal, or a ticket to a ball game. Nor will every spouse necessarily want a bottle of perfume or aftershave lotion.

Second, don't forget that NRBs should be spontaneous. If you take employees to lunch two Christmases in a row, the novelty will wear off. What's worse is that they might come to think of the Christmas lunch as part of their benefit package.

But NRBs are powerful ways to give significant Outcomes to others. And, as we've said before, Outcomes create equity and better relationship performance.

We began our discussion of managing equity in relationships by telling you that you have more control than you think you do. Perhaps now you realize that managing relationships effectively is a matter of helping others understand and change their perspectives. It's also a matter of giving important Outcomes to others through communication.

Summarized on the next page are the powers you have to manage relationships at work and at home. So change your own perspective for a few minutes and think about how satisfying and productive your relationships would be if the other people in your life used these powers with you. But you're the one who has these powers now. We wish you every success as you use them.

The Equity Power Paradigm

1. The Power of Perspective

- Identify the perspective
- Change perceptions of Inputs
- Change perceptions of Outcomes

2. The Power of Positive Expectations

- High expectations = success
- Low expectations = failure

3. The Power of Goal-setting

- Specific goals
- Realistic goals
- Participative goals

4. The Power of Performance Feedback

- Immediate feedback
- Specific feedback
- Feedback that's tied to performance
- The Hot Stove rules for negative feedback

5. The Power of Novel, Rewarding Behavior

- Add impact to feedback
- Give people a reason to talk about their accomplishments

5

Putting It All Together

We began this book with the story of a man named Charlie. Like most people, Charlie wanted productive, satisfying relationships in his life. Yet at age sixty, Charlie was alone in life, traveling to a psychiatric hospital, and thinking to himself, After All I've Done . . . Neither we nor you will probably ever know what happened to Charlie.

Charlie seemed to have more than his share of bad luck. Several of his important relationships didn't work out. But the reality is that perhaps some relationships should end:

- Some people are in such unrewarding, dissatisfying jobs that they ought to quit.
- Some people are in such difficult marriages that divorce is the right choice.

But the simple truth is that too many people are too quick to end relationships that could be saved or revitalized. As you continue to move through the multitude of relationships in your own life, we'll leave you with a few final thoughts.

First, remember that the **Equity Factor** is the single most important principle for understanding relationships. In our discussion of Entitleds and Benevolents, you learned why some people give no more than they do to relationships at work and at home and why others give so much.

Second, we've examined the process called perception and discovered that it's fragile and often unpredictable, but most critical. Because perceptions are all that count in relationships.

Third, we've explored four reasons why equity in relationships is difficult to manage:

- **The Wrong Psychological Currency**
- **Trust Bankruptcy**
- **Hidden Expectations**
- **Stamp Collecting**

Finally, to help you become a better relationship manager, we've identified five powers you have for building equity in your relationships. The **Equity Power Paradigm** offers practical solutions to relationship problems by helping to change the perspectives others have and by giving them the relationship Outcomes they want and need.

But despite the strategies that are available to all of us, too many people are only surviving in relationships that could be far more productive and fulfilling. Clearly, there's a difference between surviving and winning in relationships. This difference is frequently only a slight edge.

Achieving the "Edge of Excellence" in Relationships

Edwin Moses, a track star who runs the 400-meter hurdles, has won two Olympic gold medals, one in 1976 and one in 1984. And from 1977 to 1987 Moses won 122 consecutive races. Yet his fastest time, a world record 47.02 seconds, is only *hundredths* of a second faster than other world-class hurdlers. When his incredible string of victories was broken in the summer of 1987, he lost the race by only seven-hundredths of a second. But for ten years he maintained an edge . . . an edge that kept him a winner.

Each spring in Athens, Georgia, there is a bicycle race called the Athens Twilight Criterium. Professional bike riders come to Athens from all over the world to compete in this whirlwind race through the city's downtown. We're always amazed that the difference between winning and losing in this approximately 40-mile race is only a small one . . . a slight edge.

During one recent year, the Criterium attracted more than a hundred cyclists. The winner, a young man from Boulder, Colorado, named Davis Phinney, finished the race in 1 hour, 31 minutes, and 30 seconds. His average speed was just over 25 miles per hour—on a bicycle!

Yet twenty-one other cyclists completed the race within 45 seconds of Phinney. Think about that for a few moments—after a 40-mile bike race only 45 seconds separated the top twenty-two finishers! In fact, at the end of the race, only 4.5 *feet* separated Phinney from the second-, third-, and fourth-place riders!

You can probably think of other situations in which the difference between winning and losing was only a split second, a fraction of an inch, a slight margin. Great athletes, great business leaders, and other successful people seem to have this edge . . . what we call the Edge of Excellence.

Somehow these winners get a small jump at the start, exert more effort during the race, or perhaps have a reservoir of strength that allows them to lunge toward the finish. And the distance between them and the losers is often quite small, but discernible. In fact, this small but discernible difference is all that separates them from the rest of the pack . . . the people who merely survive.

The Edge of Excellence applies just as well to managing relationships in your life. Working for the same organization for thirty years or staying married to the same person for fifty years doesn't guarantee that the relationship is either productive or happy. Many people confuse surviving and winning.

What separates productive, satisfying relationships from those in which people seek only to survive is the edge that effective relationship managers have. And in relationships this edge is a small but discernible change in your own behavior, but a change that greatly influences people around you. A small change is what separates relationship winners from relationship survivors.

The strategies we've presented here don't require major changes in your behavior toward others. In fact, our message to you can be summarized in three ways:

1. APPROACHING RELATIONSHIPS
You move through literally hundreds of relationships during your life. Some of your relationships are permanent, while others are only temporary. And some are clearly more important than others. In fact, you'll find that most of the satisfaction you feel in life comes from no more than about 20% of your relationships. So focus your attention for a few moments on how you approach these important life relationships.

As you approach major relationships, recognize the power of the Equity Factor: people give to get. And by giving the right psychological currency—the Outcomes that others want—you'll be on the winning side of productive, satisfying relationships. So change the old adage in your life from:

It Is More Blessed to Give Than to Receive

to . . .

It Is Blessed Both to Give _and_ to Receive.

2. MANAGING RELATIONSHIPS

As you manage relationships in your life, recognize the relationship powers you have:

- **The Power of Perspective**
- **The Power of Positive Expectations**
- **The Power of Goal-setting**
- **The Power of Performance Feedback**
- **The Power of Novel, Rewarding Behaviors**

These powers won't guarantee total perfection in your relationships. But they _will_ make you a better manager of relationships because they provide you ways of increasing Outcomes for others. And increasing Outcomes for others will result in increased Outcomes for you.

Additionally, the powers will increase the amount of relationship trust you experience. They'll help you give the right psychological currencies to others, while helping to overcome problems with your own and others' hidden expectations. They'll reduce the collecting and counting of stamps in your relationships. But above all, they'll help you to help others get more from their relationship with you. So change the adage in your life from:

**Do Unto Others as You Would Have
Them Do unto You**

to . . .

**Do Unto Others as *They* Would Have
You Do unto *Them*.**

3. APPRECIATING RELATIONSHIPS

Finally, as you come to understand and appreciate the really important relationships in your life, both at work and at home, we hope that what you've learned here will help you become a real winner in relationships. But most of all we hope that what we've presented here will enable both you and others in your relationships to say less often:

"After All I've Done for You"

and say more often . . .

"Look What *We Can Do* . . . for Each Other."

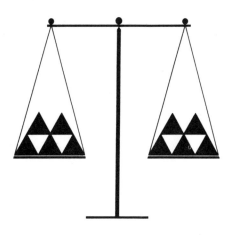

Notes

We've drawn from a variety of useful sources in compiling ideas and data for this book.

CHARLIE'S STORY

Data on people quitting their jobs were taken from the Bureau of Labor Statistics.

Data about how effective people think they can be on the job were taken from a 1983 Public Agenda Foundation survey. Our own surveys confirm these findings.

Divorce statistics were drawn from the *Statistical Abstracts of the United States*.

Statistics on teen-age runaways were taken from *U.S. News and World Report*, January 17, 1983.

I. THE EQUITY FACTOR

Aristotle's discussion of the notion of exchange can be found in his *Nicomachean Ethics*. Cambridge, Massachusetts: Harvard University Press, 1926 translation.

The quote by Adam Smith is taken from his *Wealth of Nations*. New York: Modern Library, Inc., originally published in 1776.

A detailed discussion of the Kula Ring is in Bronislaw Malinowski, *Argonauts of the Western Pacific.* London: Routledge and Kegan Paul, 1922.

Summaries of research about the effects of equity and inequity in organizations can be found in John B. Miner, *Theories of Organizational Behavior,* Hinsdale, Illinois: Dryden Press, 1980, and in Richard T. Mowday, "Equity Theory Predictions of Behavior in Organizations," in Richard M. Steers and Lyman W. Porter, eds., *Motivation and Work Behavior,* 3d ed., New York: McGraw-Hill, 1983.

For information on the equity in interpersonal relationships, see Elaine Walster, Ellen Berscheid, and Lillian Walster, "New Directions in Equity Research," in Leonard Berkowitz and Elaine Walster, eds., *Advances in Experimental Social Psychology.* New York: Academic Press, 1976.

The problem of identifying "comparison others" is summarized well in Richard T. Mowday, "Equity Theory Predictions of Behavior in Organizations."

The study of professors and their unsolicited Christmas cards can be found in Phillip R. Kunz and Michael Woolrott, "Season's Greetings from My Status to Yours," *Social Science Research,* 1976 (5).

The study of baseball players and equity is reported in Robert G. Lord and Jeffrey A. Hohenfeld, "Longitudinal Field Assessment of Equity Effects on the Performance of Major League Baseball Players," *Journal of Applied Psychology,* 1979, vol. 64.

We have reported some early findings on this notion of Equity Sensitivity in Richard C. Huseman, John D. Hatfield, and Edward W. Miles, "Test for Individual Perceptions of Job Equity: Some Preliminary Findings," *Percep-*

tual and Motor Skills, 1985, vol. 61. We also present a detailed discussion of Equity Sensitivity in "A New Perspective on Equity Theory: The Equity Sensitivity Construct," *Academy of Management Review*, 1987, no. 2.

The study of preschool children and gift-giving was reported by Marilyn Bradbard in *Psychological Reports*, vol. 56, no. 3.

2. EYE OF THE PERCEIVER

The story of the prince and the magician is adapted from John Fowles, *The Magus*. Boston: Little, Brown and Company, 1977.

Huxley's notion of how powerful our perceptual skills are was taken from Aldous Huxley, *The Doors of Perception, and Heaven and Hell*. New York: Harper and Row, 1956.

Our data on physical limitations to perception were taken from several sources, including David E. Davis, *Integral Animal Behavior*, New York: Macmillan Company, 1966; Matthew Alpern, Merle Lawrence, and David Wolsk, *Sensory Processes*, Belmont, California: Brooks/Cole Publishing Company, 1967; and Willard R. Zemlin, *Speech and Hearing Science*, Englewood Cliffs, New Jersey: Prentice-Hall, 1968.

The discussion of turkeys and skunks is adapted from M. W. Fox, *Concepts in Ethology: Animal and Human Behavior*. Minneapolis: University of Minnesota Press, 1974.

Data on skin cancer, auto accidents, smoking, and shark attacks are from the National Bureau of Health Statistics.

3 . WHY EQUITY IN RELATIONSHIPS IS
DIFFICULT TO MANAGE

The Center for Creative Leadership study is reported in "What Makes for Executive Success," *Psychology Today*, February 1983.

The Boston University study of trust was reported in the May 16, 1987, issue of *USA Today*.

The average duration of marriages in this country was taken from the *New York Times*, February 7, 1985.

The term "idiosyncratic credit" is taken from E. P. Hollander, "Conformity, Status, and Idiosyncrasy Credit," *Psychological Review*, 1958, no. 65.

4 . MANAGING EQUITY TO GET
THE RESULTS YOU WANT FROM RELATIONSHIPS

The poem about the blind men visiting the elephant is entitled "The Blind Men and the Elephant." It was written by John G. Saxe.

Using a worm to cure toothaches is an old story. We found it in a book that contains a classic study of the Pygmalion Effect in schools: Robert Rosenthal and Lenore Jacobson, *Pygmalion in the Classroom*. New York: Holt, Rinehart and Winston, 1968.

Eliza Doolittle's words are taken from G. B. Shaw, *Pygmalion*. London: Max Reinhardt, Constable, 1958.

A review of studies of the Pygmalion Effect is in Dov Eden, "Self-Fulfilling Prophecy as a Management Tool," *Academy of Management Review*, 1984, no. 1.

The Maryland firm that quoted Goethe in its annual report is Preston Trucking Company. See Robert Levering, Milton Moskowitz, and Michael Katz, *The 100 Best*

Companies to Work for in America. New York: Plume Books, 1985.

Information on birth order, achievement, and expectations can be found in Kevin Leman, *The Birth Order Book*, Fleming H. Russell Company, 1984.

An excellent review and application of goal-setting theory is in Edwin Locke, *Goal-Setting: A Motivational Technique That Works!* Englewood Cliffs, New Jersey: Prentice-Hall, 1984.

Data on divorced people remarrying within five years are taken from the *New York Times*, February 7, 1985.

For further discussion of Douglas McGregor's Hot Stove Rules, see Leon D. Boncarosky, "Guidelines to Corrective Discipline," *Personnel Journal*, October 1979.

Statistics on hunger in America are taken from *Christianity Today*, November 8, 1985, and *U.S. News and World Report*, December 19, 1983.